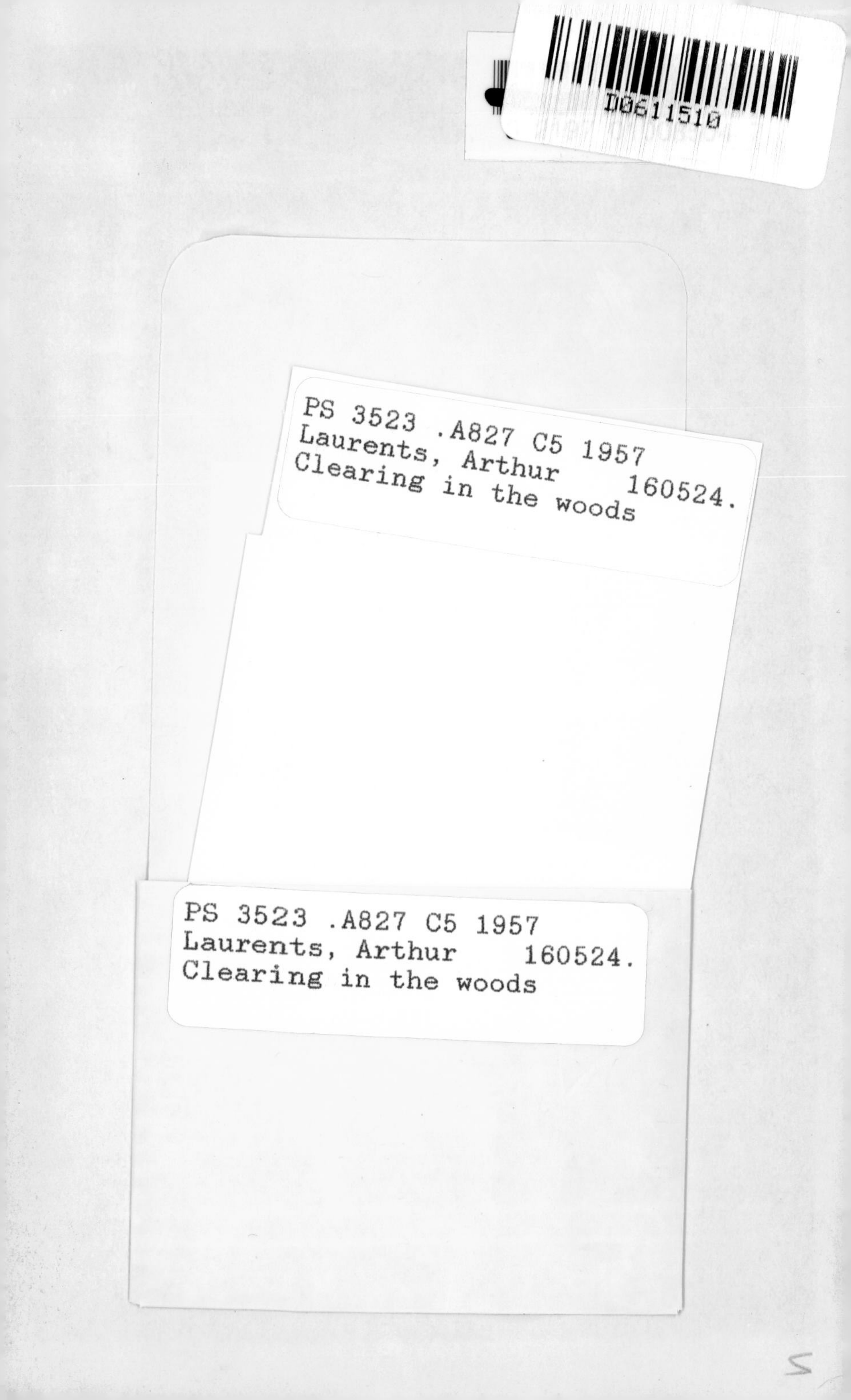

PS 3523 .A827 C5 1957
Laurents, Arthur 160524.
Clearing in the woods

A CLEARING IN THE WOODS

Random House, New York

A CLEARING IN THE WOODS

A play by ARTHUR LAURENTS

Photographs by courtesy of Vandamm

MANUFACTURED IN THE
UNITED STATES OF AMERICA

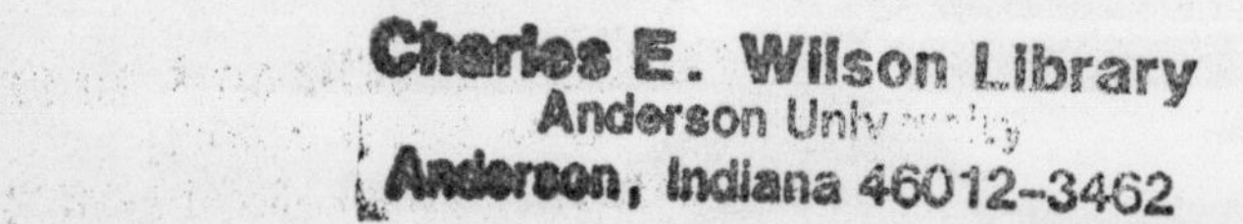

To Nora Kaye

PREFACE

Truth is always an excitement. In the theatre, the discovery of a truth can be a magical adventure made through wondrous illusion and lyric distortion. While the same discovery can of course be made through facsimiles of reality, the urge to soar above the confines of naturalistic theatre is more evident with each new production—even if only in the skeleton-walled settings now used so regularly for otherwise realistic plays. Other than Thornton Wilder, few playwrights, even in the musical field, have sought a freedom in form to attain the heightened theatricality we all seem to be seeking. Instead, formlessness is often substituted for new form (a sequence of scenes loosely strung together on a cord of mood and character); theatricality is largely supplied by extravagant violence or sensational subject matter; and truth is usually limited to the theme of eternal loneliness: man is lonely at birth, at death, even in love.

The loneliness afoot in this country must be staggering—unless only writers and their lovers are lonely—but I do not believe it a natural or inevitable state of man. I think the man who is lonely is the man who is lonely with himself because he has not accepted himself for the imperfect human being he is. Until he makes that difficult acceptance (and so many of us are startlingly unaware that we have not), he cannot feel very much, he cannot give very much, he cannot have very much. This is the theme of *A Clearing in the Woods,* and because psychiatry has instituted an awareness of this too popular problem, some have described the play as the psychoanalysis of a woman. That is foolish: what psychiatry discovered was not the problem but an effective technique for solving it. Moreover, I do not have the temerity to attempt a two-hour condensation of a complex process that usually takes years.

The theme here is found where I believe the theme of any dramatic work should be found: in the story. A woman suddenly finds herself in a clearing in a wood which seems familiar. Various people turn up, including three girls of different ages whom she does not recognize even though they recognize her and joyously announce their pleasure that she will now take care of them. At first, these girls merely confuse the woman; then they irritate her; then they goad her into doing things she hates. Finally furious, she attempts to drive them away, but at that moment they trap her and force her to the realization that they are she. This is the first act. In the second, the woman is led to the moment of choice: whether to continue fighting these girls who are less perfect than she would have them be and thus to live in perpetual torment, or whether to accept them as they are and thus be able to move onward.

The story is simple and straightforward; it is non-realistic and that is why the play is non-realistic. For no matter how many rules the play breaks, it adheres strongly to two classic tenets. The first is that content determines form. Certainly my own wish to see a theatre curtain rise on a play that floats, rather than on one that is earthbound, pushed my thoughts toward an idea such as this. But it was that idea which determined the form; it could not be otherwise.

The second rule observed is that of the unity of time, place and action. The play does not have flashbacks; it is not a dream or a nightmare or an hallucination; it does not take place in the mind of a woman. To seek some such explanation is to seek a realistic approach, to cling to naturalism because it is familiar and, thus, safe. But the action occurs only in the clearing in the woods and precisely in the sequence related.

There are two sharp departures in dramatic technique. Unlike most plays with the element of fantasy, this one does not have symbols, ghosts or vagaries for characters. They are all individual human beings, even the three girls. Even the character called George who openly remarks that he is several people. Although he does represent several men the heroine dallied with, and although as such he might be termed symbolic, he is written as a distinct individual and it is as such that he must be played. The woman must accept him as such and take his remark as a joke: its double meaning is for the audience, not for her.

The other departure is that, again unlike most plays, this one has no offstage life. With the single exception of one sexual moment, everything that happens, happens or is said onstage. The characters are aware only of the events that happen as they happen, or the words that are said as they are said; they know only of themselves what the audience knows. (Less, in one instance: the audience will know the identity of the three girls long before the woman does.)

An example: during the first half, the woman describes an attempt at suicide. Normally, an actress playing such a role would carry awareness of the attempt within her from her first entrance. Here, she should discover the attempt only as she tells it. Why? Because each scene is a scene of discoveries which the actors must make simultaneously with the audience. Any memory must be recalled only at the moment it appears in the text. The secret is for the performers to play as though they are adrift in a dark forest and suddenly a great red light is turned on. Red means sex: they play sex; white means laughter: they play laughter; blue means tears: they play tears. The capacity, of course, is and must be within the character, but the force that produces action comes from outside, comes from the nature of each scene. The play must drive the actors so that they are constantly running to catch up with it.

For modern actors, so well trained in a style of realistic reactions and transitions, of subconscious motivations and deeper meanings, this will be difficult. They will want to be aware that a reconstruction of the play will give an impressionist picture of the life of a woman. But this is for the audience, not the actors; this is not how the play is written. If it is played with realistic awareness, it will be complicated and confused for the actors and thus for the audience. "Everything has a meaning, but if you look for the meaning in everything you will lose your reason," says the woman at one point. I might add: and you will lose your audience.

Like both farce and fantasy, the play establishes an unreal premise and then remains true to it. I have tried to make it clear and simple within its unreal frame; to give each scene, each character, even each line a distinct and revealed purpose. Although the play has its own logic—as, say, *Alice in Wonderland* does—it is not arbitrary. The line of action is direct. It springs from the story and it flows on the *one reality in the play: emotion.*

Every transition, progression, development stems from emotion. For example: when the woman is raging with anger against her father, the child (who is the woman at the age of ten) runs onstage and cuts the father's tie with a pair of scissors. A few moments later, the father remembers and reminds the woman that she, as a child, cut a pair of his trousers.

A realistic approach will use memory as the link between the two incidents. Obviously, the link of memory is in the scene, but it has been put there for the audience, as a bold clue to the identity of the child. For the characters, the link is emotion, one common to all three at the same moment: anger. For here, as throughout, the play is written on two levels. The first is the simple telling of the story, the events that happen, the emotions that are felt. This level is for both actors and audience. The second is the meaning and importance of each event and relationship in the total life of the woman. This is for the audience alone, to be grasped partially as the play unfolds, perhaps more during the intermission, perhaps not completely until after the final curtain. It is the first level, the simple level only, which is to be performed.

The trick, the difficulty in performing, may be the same as it was in the writing: to equate the unreal with the real: to accept that it is perfectly natural for three girls and a woman to be the same person at different ages and still to accept that all four live their own, separate existences, blending into a single whole only at the end. Difficult? Impossible? Not if we think of ourselves now and in the past: how separate and yet how together.

Although I believe our theatre shows strongly both the need and the desire to depart from the literal and the prosaic, I do not insist that every play strive for more theatricality or more lyricism or more freedom in its search for an illumination of truth. I say only that this is what I seek from myself and for myself. This is the direction I hope our theatre takes; I am eager to pursue it. *A Clearing in the Woods* was enormously difficult to write, but I was happier writing it than anything else I have attempted.

Arthur Laurents

A CLEARING IN THE WOODS *was first presented by Roger L. Stevens and Oliver Smith at the Belasco Theatre, New York City, on January 10, 1957, with the following cast:*

(AS THEY SPEAK)

VIRGINIA (THE WOMAN)	Kim Stanley
NORA (YOUNG GIRL)	Anne Pearson
JIGEE (LITTLE GIRL)	Barbara Myers
BARNEY	Onslow Stevens
GINNA (YOUNG WOMAN)	Joan Lorring
GEORGE (THE MAN)	Pernell Roberts
PETE	Robert Culp
HAZELMAE	Sybil White
THE BOY	Tom Hatcher
ANDY	Lin McCarthy

Directed by Joseph Anthony

Production designed by Oliver Smith

Costumes designed by Lucinda Ballard

Lighting by Feder

Music by Laurence Rosenthal

SCENES

The scene is a clearing in a wood. There is no time.
There are two acts.

A CLEARING IN THE WOODS

ACT ONE

ACT ONE

The play begins in darkness, with the gently sad music of nostalgia. Very slowly, light filters onto the stage, rather like summer sun invading a morning curtain of fog. There are trees: it is a clearing in a wood; a blurred outline to one side, downstage, is the porch of a summer cottage. Lemon-gray becomes tinged with a greenish hue: grass, vines, trees which have the shape of memory.

Now the figures of three girls are vaguely outlined. One leans against a tree; another, younger, sits on an old deck chair, or tree trunk; the third, a child, rests against the cottage steps. All three are softly relaxed.

Then from a distance, a woman's voice calls, "Hello! Hello!" The figures alert. The voice calls again, closer. The girls dart center, touch hands as though in a pact of agreement, and vanish into the darkness of the trees. The light continues to brighten in the clearing and a woman rushes in, wearing a soft, flowing negligee. Her look, like her hair, is slightly disheveled.

THE WOMAN

Hello—who? Hello, me. How are you? Fine! Oh, so very fine now! I'm back, back where I always ran to catch my breath.

And I *can* breathe now! I'm here, I'm— (*Suddenly stops, looking around*) But it isn't as pretty as it was. It isn't very pretty at all. (*Going to the cottage*) Am I back? Where am I? Who was I calling? (*Mounting the steps*) Andy. (*On the porch, turns, pleading*) Andy? (*Calling*) Andy? (*Silence. Then, with a wry smile*) No Andy. Which fact she knew, but knowing never yet killed hope.

(*Summer morning sunlight is drifting through the trees as the* YOUNG GIRL *appears. About seventeen, she wears attractive clothes which are somehow slightly odd.*)

THE WOMAN

Caught in the act of conversing with an old enemy: me.

YOUNG GIRL

Oh, I do it all the time!

THE WOMAN

Do you interrupt yourself with yourself?

YOUNG GIRL

Naturally!

THE WOMAN

Then we must interrupt ourselves with each other sometime. (*Descending the steps*) Good evening.

YOUNG GIRL

Good evening—and welcome, welcome home!

THE WOMAN

Then that *is* where I am.

YOUNG GIRL

Of course!

THE WOMAN

Why isn't it pretty?

YOUNG GIRL

It's wildly pretty! And we're all so glad, you don't know how glad we are that you've finally come back.

THE WOMAN

Glad? To see me? Who is so glad?

(From behind the cottage, a LITTLE GIRL *of about nine or ten appears. She is dressed very neatly, complete with little white gloves, little hat, little purse—and her clothes are somehow not quite usual. She carries a battered little toy animal. Light illuminates a torn kite captured in the trees and, perhaps, an old rope swing.)*

LITTLE GIRL

Who? Who who who?

YOUNG GIRL

Be still.

LITTLE GIRL

Why?

YOUNG GIRL

Because I tell you to.

LITTLE GIRL

(*To* THE WOMAN)

That's so typical of her. (*To the* YOUNG GIRL) Give me a reason.

YOUNG GIRL

I'm older.

LITTLE GIRL

Old old old!

YOUNG GIRL

Do as I tell you!

LITTLE GIRL

(*To* THE WOMAN)

See? Nobody ever explains, not a single thing. "Do as I tell you," that's all. Well, when I grow up, I'm going to do what *I* tell *me!*

THE WOMAN

Bravo!

LITTLE GIRL

There! Oh, I'm so glad you're back!

THE WOMAN

You, too?

LITTLE GIRL

You knew I'd be.

THE WOMAN

Did I? You're both too young to be mad. Although I suppose they *have* lowered the age limit these days.

YOUNG GIRL

I adore mad people! I'm mad myself.

LITTLE GIRL

As long as you think you are, you really aren't.

THE WOMAN

(*Oddly serious suddenly*)

That *is* true, isn't it?

YOUNG GIRL

No!

LITTLE GIRL

Yes!

Simultaneously

THE WOMAN

It is! Why are you both so glad I'm back?

YOUNG GIRL

Now you'll take care of us.

THE WOMAN

Why me?

YOUNG GIRL

He's too old to do it.

THE WOMAN

He?

LITTLE GIRL

He never did anyway.

YOUNG GIRL

No, he doesn't like us. Not really.

LITTLE GIRL

Not at all. (*To* THE WOMAN) But you do, don't you?

THE WOMAN

Like you? I don't even know you.

(*Music. The two girls look at each other and laugh.*)

YOUNG GIRL

She doesn't know herself!

LITTLE GIRL

She's Nora.

YOUNG GIRL

She's Jigee.

LITTLE GIRL

Look!

(*Takes off her glasses and puts them in her purse.*)

NORA (YOUNG GIRL)

Any excuse to take them off.

JIGEE (LITTLE GIRL)

They're just corrective.

NORA

You're squinting again.

JIGEE

It's the sun. (*To* THE WOMAN) Doesn't the sun make your eyes squinty?

THE WOMAN

Indeed it does! Particularly on my way to the office in the morning. (*Suddenly*) It *is* morning. I said, "good evening." (*To* NORA) You said, "good evening."

NORA

Why not turn time upside down if you want to? It's fun!

JIGEE

Fun fun fun!

THE WOMAN

(*A sudden cry*)

Don't!

JIGEE

(*To* NORA)

What's the matter with her? (*To* THE WOMAN) You're acting very peculiar.

THE WOMAN

I'm just tired. It's a long drive from town. Why are you here? I came back to be alone. But how can you be alone where you have been before?

JIGEE

You don't like us. (*To* NORA) I told you she wouldn't want to take care of us.

THE WOMAN

But I don't know you.

JIGEE

See?

NORA

She's just joking. (*To* THE WOMAN) You do know us and you are going to take care of us, aren't you? Say yes.

JIGEE

Please say yes, Virginia.

(*At the mention of the name, the music stops and* THE WOMAN, VIRGINIA, *moves abruptly. A pause.*)

VIRGINIA

Jigee . . . Nora . . .

NORA

(*Uncertainly*)

You were joking, weren't you?

VIRGINIA

Of course! (*With a bright smile to conceal the lie*) Of course I was joking! I do remember! Now why don't you go swimming in the cove? The water this time of the year was always like silk. Or go play up at the house: croquet! The mallets were always kept in the—

NORA

We know where they are.

JIGEE

She wants to be rid of us. I *told* you she would.

(JIGEE *begins fumbling in her purse for her glasses as a man appears on the path from the house, offstage,* VIRGINIA *indicated. Lean, tanned, crew-cut, he is an "old boy" with an infectious, charming grin which he uses to dull the edge of his remarks. He wears casual clothes with a rather bright tie, and carries a golf club.*)

VIRGINIA

Daddy! Oh, Daddy, I—

BARNEY

You cry too quickly.

VIRGINIA

I'm just so happy to see you here.

BARNEY

Where'd you think I'd be?

NORA

At the club.

BARNEY

Matter of fact, I should be. But there is always a moment to say welcome to my only offspring.

VIRGINIA

Say more than welcome. (*He looks at his watch*) Stay. Permission is granted to enter the sacred circle.

BARNEY

What?

VIRGINIA

Oh, Barney, you remember!

(*Music, as she describes a "circle" in the clearing, ending with her arms upstretched to him. He walks down past her.*)

BARNEY

Really, Virginia, that was only a silly child's rule.

NORA

It isn't silly. Even a child wants a place of her own.

JIGEE

True true true! (*Pointing to the cottage*) I want that!

BARNEY

(*Entering the clearing*)

You can't have it. And those glasses are meant to be worn.

JIGEE

Why?

BARNEY

So when you grow up you won't need 'em and you'll be pretty.

VIRGINIA

She's pretty now.

BARNEY

Glasses don't exactly help, Virginia.

JIGEE

Why do I have to be pretty?

BARNEY

Because you're a girl.

JIGEE

But why?

BARNEY

(*Amiably*)

Because I say so.

JIGEE

That again!

BARNEY

Pretty girls are happy girls.

VIRGINIA

Happy girls are pretty girls.

NORA

Touché!

BARNEY

(*To* NORA)

Honey, you'll be happier if you keep in line with what other people think.

NORA

(*To* VIRGINIA)

Just yesterday he said: Learn to think for yourself and stand on your own two feet.

BARNEY

Can't you do both?

VIRGINIA

Oh, yes: with two heads.

(*All the girls laugh.* BARNEY *takes a full swing with his club.*)

BARNEY

Fore! (*With a grin, to* JIGEE) I never could be a winner around here, baby.

JIGEE

(*Primly*)

You should only say baby to infants or lady friends.

BARNEY

Pretty girls make out better than smart girls. Unless you can be both. (*To* NORA *and* JIGEE) Your mother would never let anyone but me see her reading.

VIRGINIA

Yes, Daddy, I know.

BARNEY

(*Poking at her negligee with his golf club*)

She was partial to things soft and floating, too. Of course, I don't exactly recall her wearing one down here.

VIRGINIA

Oh. Well, I didn't know where I was going to wind up when I left town last night. I—suddenly needed some place to unwind. Overworking, hard work . . . Well, not really. Parties have become the hardest, whether giving or going. Last week, I cooked a complete East Indian dinner for ten people and left in the middle. Of course, Mother—Well, this is soft and cool, and it was too hot for sleeping in town last night . . . Well, I didn't know where I was heading. I said that. (*Finally*) No, Mother would not have made the error of wearing this.

NORA

I think it's a dream

VIRGINIA

I wish it were.

NORA

But it is. It's very pretty!

VIRGINIA

Oh—thank you.

BARNEY

What's the difference? You're *here!*

VIRGINIA

You *are* glad!

BARNEY

I just hope you stay long enough for us to have a good talk.

JIGEE

A good long talk.

NORA

Long enough for him to lead up to the reason he's glad you're here.

BARNEY

You two scoot out of here! Go on, get!

NORA

He has a reason.

JIGEE

He always has.

VIRGINIA

Go away.

NORA

You know he has.

VIRGINIA

Go away!

JIGEE

Foolish foolish foolish.

(*She follows* NORA *into the trees, defiantly taking off her glasses just as she disappears into the darkness.*)

BARNEY

I don't have a reason. You're just always suspicious.

VIRGINIA

It would only be suspicious if you had no reason. Even strangers seem to know that.

BARNEY

What? Who are the strangers?

VIRGINIA

Tell me.

BARNEY

Tell me: who.

VIRGINIA

You don't count children.

BARNEY

What do you mean?

VIRGINIA

Nothing. Everything has a meaning, but look for the meaning in everything and you can lose your reason. Lose yours, Daddy. Your reason for being glad to see me.

BARNEY

What strangers? Virginia, are you ill?

VIRGINIA

(*Gaily*)

Was I ever well? Did the Black Fairy ever leave my cradle? (*Quietly*) I am in bad need of a friend. Are you my good friend, Daddy?

BARNEY

Certainly.

VIRGINIA

Then you are glad to see me!

BARNEY

You can't live on sentiment, Virginia—

VIRGINIA

If you do have a reason, please tell it to me.

BARNEY

You know that property I gave you as a wedding present? You're divorced now, you're not doing a thing with the land—

VIRGINIA

Those girls were right: you did have a reason.

BARNEY

It wasn't my idea, you understand, but my lawyers suggested—

VIRGINIA

Barney, I don't care about lawyers and property!

BARNEY

You'd better begin to care. Prices are going up, sky-high. You don't understand these things the way your mother did, but—

VIRGINIA

What prices are going up sky-high, Barney? Golf balls or whiskey?

BARNEY

That is unfair. I ration my drinks now and you know it. I am merely trying to provide for our needs—

VIRGINIA

That need, I can provide for myself.

BARNEY

Can you?

VIRGINIA

Yes!

BARNEY

With what?

VIRGINIA

With what I earn.

BARNEY

Ha!

VIRGINIA

An executive assistant makes—

BARNEY

Fancy title for secretary—

VIRGINIA

You think that because I'm a woman!

BARNEY

Your back goes up like a jack-in-the-box!

VIRGINIA

Two people were needed for that job before I took it over! I'm good! But that's something you'll never believe.

BARNEY

If you say so, I believe it.

(Swings his golf club. She looks at him.)

VIRGINIA

Why do you always need a reason for being glad to see me?!

BARNEY

If you were your father—*(Swings again)* you'd need a reason.

(A bright voice calls out "Hi!" and the YOUNG WOMAN *comes up into the clearing from behind the cottage. About twenty-six, she wears a terrycloth robe over a wet bathing suit and has sunglasses on. She is drying her hair with a towel that she eventually winds into a turban.)*

YOUNG WOMAN

Throw open the welcome doors and call out a great big "good evening!"

VIRGINIA

(Happily)

Morning!

YOUNG WOMAN

(Takes off dark glasses)

So it is. My eyes hurt. From working last night or from the sea this morning? Or simply from belonging to me?

VIRGINIA

I often have hangovers from me.

YOUNG WOMAN

This time, let's really try to get rid of them. Glad you're back. (*On this, she and* VIRGINIA *make the same gesture simultaneously*) I'm Ginna.

VIRGINIA

Oh . . . Of course.

GINNA (YOUNG WOMAN)
(*Misreading* VIRGINIA'S *curious behavior*)

Has he been upsetting you? (*Turns to* BARNEY) Sly comparisons to a mother who was perfection—(*To* VIRGINIA) or has he been belittling your work?

VIRGINIA

The lady knows you well, Barney.

BARNEY

Her understanding of men is on a par with yours.

GINNA

I understand you.

BARNEY

As you do your husband.

GINNA

No. Pete is not quite as simple.

BARNEY

We have a game scheduled. Where is the lad?

GINNA

Down at the cove. (*To* VIRGINIA) It's years since he was king of the campus, but there he is: swimming his forty or fifty laps to keep in shape.

BARNEY

What's so wrong with the boy wanting to remain in shape?

GINNA

What is wrong, Sir Crew-Cut, is a man wanting to remain a boy. Why doesn't he try keeping his head in shape?

BARNEY

Perhaps he's too busy ducking jabs from you.

GINNA

(*Smiles wryly*)

Score one for your side.

VIRGINIA

Echoes.

BARNEY

(*To* GINNA)

Let him be.

GINNA

Be what? I wish I knew—for his sake.

BARNEY

Really for his sake?

GINNA

Yes! As you well know, Virginia.

VIRGINIA

I don't even know Pete.

GINNA

Understandable. Pete doesn't know himself. Barney, spare a moment from your athletics. Surprise her. Be nice, for once. I have to attack that very large mountain on my very small desk.

BARNEY

Another day, another cause.

GINNA

(*To* VIRGINIA)

Same Barney, same joke.

BARNEY

Now, Ginna, I don't mean to run down these do-good organizations—

GINNA

Then don't reduce people who are trying, to a snide little country club phrase! And don't ridicule my work because I'm a woman. The work I am doing may not matter fifty miles from here, but I am not sitting at a bridge table! The job is neither pleasant nor easy, but to me it's exciting and useful, and someone has to do it! (*In a second, her flare-up dies and she grins. To* VIRGINIA) Wow! Would you say I get a bit carried away?

VIRGINIA

Well . . .

BARNEY

Virginia can't answer. She has a real job now.

VIRGINIA

Thank you.

GINNA

Well, comes the revolution, I will not only have a real job, I will be real.

BARNEY

It won't satisfy you until you're different.

GINNA

Ah, but from whom?

BARNEY

Us ordinary people.

GINNA

Now I thought you were the one who always said: Be an individual. Either you—(VIRGINIA *joins in*)—stand on your own two feet or—(*They stop.* GINNA *laughs*) Oh, dear, oh, dear, the echoes. Maddening, aren't they?

VIRGINIA

They're getting to be.

GINNA

(*Indicating* BARNEY)

And he's such a charmer. Why do I tussle with him?

VIRGINIA

Why ask me?

GINNA

Always the optimist: I keep hoping you'll have the answer.

VIRGINIA

Answers? Fresh out.

GINNA

Me—I'm stale out.

(*As she drifts off up the path, the nostalgic music returns for a bit.*)

VIRGINIA

Are the woods full of them? Is there one for every tree? Are they day-blooming or do they breed better after sundown?

BARNEY

What?

VIRGINIA

They swing in and out like doors!

BARNEY

Memories do.

VIRGINIA

I meant those girls.

BARNEY

(*Puts down his club*)

What in the world is the matter with you?

VIRGINIA

With me, it's what is the matter with the world. See? I tumble words, but they were all upside down anyway. (*Bewildered*) Somehow, as we grow up, the meanings change. I don't mean to upset you. Do what you will with the property.

BARNEY

Never mind. What's bothering you?

VIRGINIA

Nothing.

BARNEY

You could tell me. But you never do. You never come to see me. After your divorce, you moved out and you haven't spent one night here since.

VIRGINIA

It's difficult, Barney, living in town, working . . .

(*A pause. He looks at her, then loosens his tie angrily, turns away, then back.*)

BARNEY

Last night I dreamt I was dead, laid out in the dining room up at the house. The windows were wide open to the rain and the wind. You wouldn't believe a dead man could get cold and wet. He can; I did. No one to shut those windows. You wouldn't believe a dead man could be thinking. He can; I was. I was thinking: "I've never done anything: all right. I've never even done one small thing I really wanted to: also all right: a waste—no tragedy . . . But I've never made anyone happy." (*Pause*) Your mother wouldn't let me, either.

VIRGINIA

I am not Mother!

BARNEY

No.

VIRGINIA

And you've told me that dream before.

BARNEY

It's a recurrent dream! (*Belligerently*) Most people are glad, very glad, to see me. I entertain them. That means I make them happy for a short time, anyway, doesn't it?

VIRGINIA

(*As he picks up his club*)

If you wanted to, you could . . .

BARNEY

What?

VIRGINIA

I said—(*Clears her throat*)—if you wanted to, you could.

BARNEY

Could what?

VIRGINIA

(*Almost choking, it is so difficult to say the words*)
—Help—me . . .

BARNEY

Oh, you're one of the strong ones, Virginia. They never need—

VIRGINIA

(*Interrupting angrily*)
I am not strong! And I am exhausted from pretending to be! I am human; I am vulnerable; I hurt!

BARNEY

Oh? Bad luck with love?

VIRGINIA

That pain has an identity—not mine. Mine is one enormous zero in the dead center of nothing! I awake by reflex, not desire. I am so strong that four days ago I went to my office, to the same door I have been opening for over three years—(*He has begun, nervously, to swing his club. She strides over*) The door was not locked, Barney—(*She grabs the club from him*) but I could not open it. (*Drops the club on the ground*) I could not make my hand touch the knob! I pretended to be searching my purse as one of the secretaries opened the door for me. That day, and the next and the next after that, I sat, staring at the gilded sign that had been painted for me. When the room was entered, I picked up a telephone and recited jargon. When alone, I began staring at the open window . . . Then I dropped a piece of paper out, then a cup, then an ashtray. My office is on the sixteenth floor now. Yesterday I took off my shoes and crouched on the window sill. How long? Sense of time and place have gone. Then one of the phones rang, shrilled like an air-raid alarm—and I ran. To my apartment? Because then I was standing in the ugly light of the medicine chest with a handful of neon-colored sleeping pills. I think I screamed—and ran: down halls and stairs. Then riding, driving down a houseless road that stopped at a footpath through trees. The path, I knew; the path brought me here: home. (*Cries out*) Why isn't it pretty here? (*Smiles*) Probably because that absurd feeling has followed me.

BARNEY

What feeling?

VIRGINIA

(*Lightly*)

That something terrible is going to happen to me.

BARNEY

Like what?

VIRGINIA

It has no shape.

BARNEY

Now, how can you be afraid and not know of what?

VIRGINIA

Ah, that's the very best kind of fear. Your blood can stop at the sound of a leaf. Your heart—(*Stops, whirls toward the trees*) Someone is listening!

BARNEY

Where?

VIRGINIA

I saw color in there: a dress: one of those girls!

BARNEY

What difference if they listen.

VIRGINIA

What difference?

BARNEY

Don't you like them?

VIRGINIA

Like them? I don't even know—(*Corrects herself*) I don't mind them. (*Laughs*) Maybe they are the terrible thing that's going to happen to me. But they've happened: I've met them. They remind me of things I used to do. They're confusing, slightly irritating, but nothing terrible. (*A moment. Quietly, to him*) Well, Doctor?

BARNEY

(*Grins*)

Well, madam, speaking impersonally—

VIRGINIA

Please don't.

(*Now that she has finally asked him for help, he is thrown. During the following, he grins, shrugs, yanks at his tie, pulls it off, plays with it, finally lets it drop from his fingers.*)

BARNEY

Whatever happened to that beau of yours who *was* a doctor? I liked him.

VIRGINIA

Andy wasn't a doctor the way you mean and this has nothing to do with him.

BARNEY

He worked in a hospital, didn't he?

VIRGINIA

I haven't seen him in two years.

BARNEY

I had the impression that he was going to be husband number two.

VIRGINIA

Your impression was wrong.

BARNEY

All right. I'm just trying to explore all the avenues. Logically. Now it isn't love, so . . . it must be overwork. Virginia, I'm sure that all you need is a good night's sleep.

VIRGINIA

But does sleep need me? What happens to the night when I am not in it? My bed has sprawled unmade for a week; my apartment has gone to weed; the extra room remains unfurnished. I loathe that apartment and yet I cannot get myself to move out. It's like being unable to open that office door: I want to but—(*He looks at his watch. She laughs*) You're late for your game.

BARNEY

You ask for help only to expose my inadequacy. God wouldn't satisfy you! (*She picks up his club and hands it to him*) I recognize your ailment because I, too, suffered from it. Just one more birdie, I'd say, then no more drink. I never made the birdie—(*Grins*) so I always took the drink. Until I *realized* I was never going to make it.

VIRGINIA

Then you gave up trying: you quit.

BARNEY

You would look at it that way.

VIRGINIA

And you still drink.

BARNEY

Realistically! And I did not quit trying! I merely faced my limitations like a mature individual.

VIRGINIA

All right, Barney.

BARNEY

I *could* help you, but not when all you tell me is hogwash about crouching on window sills—

VIRGINIA

That happened!

BARNEY

(*Continuing through her interruption*)

—Crazy fears, feeling like a zero! By God, even the *problems* of other people don't satisfy you! As usual, you have to be different!

VIRGINIA

Don't resent me because you gave up: making the hours go, with lawyers and papers that can take care of each other—

BARNEY

The estate would dwindle away without me! It's an important responsibility.

VIRGINIA

Perhaps. But don't you really want more of a part in living? I do!

BARNEY

You'll never get it either! We're the ordinary same as everyone else!

VIRGINIA

I'm not! Nor will I be!

BARNEY

Take it from me, you are!

VIRGINIA

Go on, your nine holes are waiting!

BARNEY

I'm still good for eighteen—and you be damned!

(*As he turns and strides angrily off, up the path toward the house, there is music, and* JIGEE *runs into the clearing with a little red suitcase from which she takes a pair of scissors. She picks up* BARNEY'S *tie from the ground and cuts it.*)

VIRGINIA

What are you doing?

JIGEE

He was mean to you. (*With a snip for each word*) Mean mean—

VIRGINIA

(*Grabbing the pieces*)

Stop it!

JIGEE

(*Holding up one piece*)
Like his tongue. Don't you wish it were?

VIRGINIA

You're a bad little girl.

JIGEE

I'm *not* bad! You have no gratitude!

VIRGINIA

Gratitude?!

JIGEE

I heard. I eavesdrop, you know.

VIRGINIA

You had better go home.

JIGEE

Oh, Virginia! I *am* home!
(*The music stops.*)

VIRGINIA

Go home!

JIGEE

I don't mean to frighten you. I want you to love me and take care of me. I don't have anyone else, do I? (*She hears something, stops and listens, then throws the shears across the grass*) Don't tattle on me. If you care one little bit, you won't—

(*She darts out of the clearing as* BARNEY *is seen through the trees, coming down the path.* VIRGINIA *crams the pieces of tie in her pocket. Unnoticed is the one piece which* JIGEE *held and dropped on the grass.*)

BARNEY

(*Entering*)

I lost my good-luck tie.

(*Begins to search the ground.*)

VIRGINIA

Find it and lend it to me.

(*She sees the piece on the ground and goes casually toward it.*)

BARNEY

Wasn't I wearing it?

VIRGINIA

Not when you left.

(*Covers the piece with her foot.*)

BARNEY

I refuse to become absent-minded: I'm not old enough.

VIRGINIA

Neither am I, but my refusal was refused.

BARNEY

I recall tying it three times this morning. I always do that when I'm going to play with—(*Stops. Slowly picks up the garden shears*) Years ago, I had a new pair of plus fours. Someone cut them to shreds . . . What's under your foot?

VIRGINIA

China.

(*He throws the shears to the ground, close enough to frighten her into moving. The piece of tie is bold on the grass.*)

BARNEY

All the years that have gone by and still—

VIRGINIA

I didn't cut it.

BARNEY

Feel as you feel, but admit it!

VIRGINIA

I did not cut that tie.

BARNEY

Any more than the pants.

VIRGINIA

No!

BARNEY

Then who did? Who could you care enough about to protect?

JIGEE

(*Appearing*)

Me! And don't you talk like that to her!

VIRGINIA

No. She didn't, she—

BARNEY

(*To* JIGEE)

You knew it was my lucky tie. You knew it was my favorite.

VIRGINIA

Barney, it's a tie!

BARNEY

Don't call me Barney. I'm your father! (*To* JIGEE) Why did you do it?

JIGEE

(*Defiance fading*)

You weren't nice, you were mean . . .

BARNEY

Eavesdropping again.

JIGEE

. . . Yes.

BARNEY

You must enjoy making me angry, you do it so well.

JIGEE

(*Near tears*)

I didn't mean to hurt you.

VIRGINIA

Barney, she's a child!

BARNEY

A bad child.

JIGEE

(*Crying*)

I'm not! I didn't mean it, I love you!

BARNEY

So I see.

JIGEE

I do! Better than the world!

VIRGINIA

Answer her!

JIGEE

(*Clinging to him*)

Spank me. Do *something!*

VIRGINIA

Daddy!

(BARNEY *moves away from the child.*)

JIGEE

You don't care if I love you or not!

BARNEY

Not when you're bad, no.

JIGEE

Not ever! Never!

(*She runs into the trees.*)

VIRGINIA

Jigee!

BARNEY

Let me handle her. I know kids: they cry all the time.

VIRGINIA

She is not crying now.

BARNEY

Because she knows she was bad.

VIRGINIA

Anyone can love a good child, Barney.

BARNEY

Including me.

VIRGINIA

She's *not* bad. She cut the tie only to get attention.

BARNEY

(*Grins*)

Next time, she'll cut my throat. That'll get a lot of attention.

VIRGINIA

Your jokes are sour! Years and years ago, not long after Mother died, I wrote you a letter that you still quote as a great joke. I was even younger than that child. And I was in love with you then.

(*The lighting begins to turn to haze around them. Nostalgic music is heard.*)

BARNEY

You should have loved your mother more.

VIRGINIA

You loved her so much, how could I? She was always out with you or away with you. You were both away on one of those trips when she died. (*He turns away*) When you returned, you told me she was still away. It was only long after, after I had accepted her absence, that I learned the truth from a schoolteacher. Then—I hopefully stole Mother's old wedding ring. But even though she was gone, you were still trying to find her.

BARNEY

(*Rattling in embarrassment*)

She loved me completely: you were a child, you didn't understand: what letter do I quote as a joke?

VIRGINIA

"Dearest Daddy. You never want me around because I am not pretty. Therefore, I am a stepchild and so I am running away. Your loving daughter, Virginia."

BARNEY

Don't you think that's funny coming from a kid of seven or eight?

VIRGINIA

I put it on your desk and sat in my room with the door open, waiting for you. Company came. You read them the letter.

Everyone laughed. You called to the maid, "Pack a bag for Miss Virginia." She put me out on the verandah, with my little red suitcase. A clear, bright autumn day. I pull the shades on days like that now. Oh, she gave me a sandwich, too, an apple and a pear. I didn't know where to go. Then I heard everyone inside laugh again, you loudest of all. I rang the bell and the maid opened the door. "I thought you were running away," she said, and I said, "Just because he wants me to, I won't."

BARNEY

I was watching from behind the curtains. I wouldn't have let you get very far.

VIRGINIA

Why didn't you say something when I came in? Why didn't you even look at me? Why did you laugh? (*The music ends; the lighting returns*) That night, I cut your new trousers.

BARNEY

(*Bewildered*)

But I've always had great success with that story. If it isn't funny, why does everyone laugh?

VIRGINIA

Don't tell it any more, Daddy. It isn't good for you to tell it.

BARNEY

I don't understand why. Now I *will* be late for my game. (*Goes toward trees, then stops*) One of these days, I'll surprise you.

VIRGINIA

Yes, Daddy. You do that.

(*He goes off as* GINNA *appears in the clearing, in a simple summer dress, and holding a man's athletic cardigan. She walks up behind* VIRGINIA, *who is sitting.*)

GINNA

(*Gently, to* VIRGINIA)

Feel better?

VIRGINIA

(*Without turning; as though talking to herself*)

I should have told him long ago or not at all. What is the good of telling someone too old to change?

GINNA

It would have been kinder to rid yourself of it through someone else.

VIRGINIA

I couldn't dare tell anyone.

GINNA

Why not?

VIRGINIA

They would know me, then.

GINNA

And not like you.

VIRGINIA

How did you know? (*Turns sharply and sees* GINNA) Another eavesdropper!

GINNA

Now, you know I've given that up.

VIRGINIA

I don't know. And how else could you know what I said to Barney?

GINNA

I would not have to eavesdrop to know that. But as it happened, I did overhear. I was passing this way to—

VIRGINIA

To eavesdrop!

GINNA

To find Pete. We had another battle royal. During them, I'm so sure everything is his fault. But afterwards—(*Holds out the cardigan she is carrying*) "Don't catch cold," I'll say.

VIRGINIA

Whose is that?

GINNA

His: Pete's.

VIRGINIA

Pete? Pete? What is Pete to me?

GINNA

What is— Virginia, sometimes you mystify me.

VIRGINIA

Then I have the advantage: you mystify me all times! And you make me frightened!

GINNA

How? Of what?

VIRGINIA

(*Backing away*)

I don't know. It's on the tip of my mind. I'm afraid that if it becomes clearer . . . Go away.

GINNA

When I heard you'd come back, I thought you'd come back to your senses, too.

VIRGINIA

Go, please . . .

GINNA

I thought you'd realized it was easier to like us. Heaven knows, I've tried like mad, but you won't, will you? You're such a fool. I'm your friend, Virginia.

VIRGINIA

Friend!

(*Unconsciously, she has picked up* JIGEE'S *toy animal.*)

GINNA

Don't you know that by now?

VIRGINIA

By now? Ah, I see! An enchanted woods, this: every second is a day, every minute is a year, every hour is love. Dear Old Friend! No, I did not know! And here is a disclosure you don't know: I am sitting on a seesaw. Yes. Two of me: one at each end. A neat trick? As an old friend, you should know I am very tricky. One of me was in mid-air before she arrived: she *knew* she was lost. But the other? (*She whispers*) The other is terrified when it is her turn to swing up there. I am terrified: of you, of all three of you, and of what you—

(*A shot rings out some distance off. They whirl in fear.* GINNA *cries softly.*)

GINNA

Pete! . . .

VIRGINIA

Andy! . . .

(*Two more shots, a little closer. The light in the clearing becomes jagged, split into shadows.* GINNA *dashes into the trees as* VIRGINIA *cries out.*)

VIRGINIA

I didn't mean it, Andy! (*Silence. Then*) Mean what? Andy who? Virginia where? Up we go, down we go! Let's you and me and Marjorie Daw swing over the trees and away! After you, Marjorie. No, after you, friend Virginia. Are you losing your marbles—or apples? Are you going off your rocker—or trolley? You see, dear ladies, there is always an alternative, always a choice. And that is a large trouble: choice, decision—

(*Through the trees comes the music of a cocktail dance band. Slowly,* VIRGINIA *backs away from the sound. It comes closer. Panicked, she would run, escape—when a whistle joins the music and into the clearing comes a jaunty man. Angular, attractive, sophisticated, he is dressed too casually for hunting. Nevertheless, he carries a shotgun, a knapsack slung over one shoulder and, in one hand, a portable radio. The light, like* VIRGINIA, *becomes bright and sunny.*)

VIRGINIA

A radio! A plain, prosaic portable radio!

THE MAN

With perishable batteries. (*Clicks it off*) Good afternoon.

VIRGINIA

And you know the time of day!

THE MAN

You've been dubious of your sanity.

VIRGINIA

Yes!

THE MAN

Relax. Touch the air; roll in the hours; look at the quiet!

VIRGINIA

You find it pretty!

THE MAN

You're too accustomed to seeing through windows. You'll find it pretty after a while.

VIRGINIA

How long did it take you? Or have you always lived here? (*Indicating the shotgun he is propping against a tree*) Are you a professional hunter?

THE MAN

Me? Dear lady, I fire that weapon, but the only thing I've ever hit was my toe. It's portable décor, a sort of virile accessory. Less trite than blue jeans, don't you think? (*She laughs*) Ah . . . it's beginning to function.

VIRGINIA

What is?

THE MAN

My only asset: Charm. Don't laugh; it really is. The trouble is charm wears thin. Sooner or later, it irritates everyone. Even me. However, if we both make the most of it while it's working—(*Quietly*)—It's working very well now, isn't it?

VIRGINIA

Very, very well.

THE MAN

Then we shall have a very, very nice time, Virginia.
(*A stab of music for a moment.*)

VIRGINIA

How do you know my name? Never mind: I should have anticipated that. (*Smiles*) At least, you're male.

THE MAN

To the best of my ability.

VIRGINIA

Nevertheless, like the others, you are glad I am back so that I now can take care of you and give you a home.

THE MAN

I have a home. Look, are you confusing me with a couple of other people?

VIRGINIA

No, I'm just confusing me.

THE MAN

We *have* met before, I swear by your favorite superstition. Only once, however, so if you don't remember me—

VIRGINIA

Once? Where? When?

THE MAN

A year or so ago, while I was still working at living in town. It was at a martini fiesta in one of those reprint apartments on ceramic avenue. I'm George.

VIRGINIA

George. Dear George, hello!

GEORGE (THE MAN)

Dear Virginia, you needn't be polite. I have an iron ego. You don't remember, but we drank great quantities, then ducked out to dinner, which we drank, then back to my place where—

VIRGINIA

Oh, I'm afraid you could be several people.

GEORGE

Oh, I'm afraid I am.

(*Again, the musical stab.*)

VIRGINIA

Up goes the seesaw.

GEORGE

Nice in mid-air, isn't it?

VIRGINIA

No.

GEORGE

Yes. It couldn't be more private: too low for planes, too high for windows. You, my girl, are frightened only because it's new.

VIRGINIA

Is that all? Tell me it is.

GEORGE

I'll tell you anything you want. I have all the answers because I am the happiest man in the world. (*Getting his knapsack*) That's fact, not charm.

VIRGINIA

Are you really?

GEORGE

Absolutely.

VIRGINIA

What's the secret?

GEORGE

It's cocktail hour. Sit down.

(*He turns on the radio and, during the following, takes a thermos and two glasses from his sack and joins her.*)

VIRGINIA

Will you tell me the secret?

GEORGE

Will you look at my mobiles?

VIRGINIA

If they are different.

GEORGE

They are.

VIRGINIA

Then away we go!

(*Sits on the grass.*)

GEORGE

In matters of this nature, I am a classicist: (*Hands her a glass*) We begin with the martini. (*Sits beside her, then pulls an imaginary lamp chain. Some light goes out behind them. The radio plays. Raises his glass*) To you.

VIRGINIA

To your secret. (*They drink*) Now.

(GEORGE *pulls another imaginary lamp chain. More light goes out. They are in a soft, sensual glow.*)

GEORGE

Now.

(*He takes her hand.*)

VIRGINIA

The secret.

GEORGE

After.

VIRGINIA

Before. (*Takes her hand away*) It's too abrupt.

GEORGE

(*Sighs*)

Haven't you read the Bible? The part that goes: At the last day on earth, thou shall account to the Lord for every pleasure thou failed to enjoy?

VIRGINIA

What Bible is that?

GEORGE

Deuteronomy, Old Testament, but concentrate on the message.

VIRGINIA

Help me. Help me forget everything before this minute.

GEORGE

Enjoyment isn't forgetting, it's making a happy memory. (*Kisses her hand*) Of love, for example.

VIRGINIA

Love or love-making?

GEORGE

(*Kissing the inside of her elbow*)

Love doesn't exist. It's a wish invented by the first author and the major source of income for all authors happily ever after.

(*He kisses her neck.*)

VIRGINIA

And the readers?

GEORGE

Read the exaggerations, look at their own lovers in horror, die of frustration.

VIRGINIA

(Laughs)

I like when you joke.

GEORGE

(Straightening up)

I was not joking.

VIRGINIA

You believe in love.

GEORGE

I do not.

VIRGINIA

(Taking his hand)

You do.

GEORGE

I believe in Nothing.

VIRGINIA

I don't believe you.

(She moves closer.)

GEORGE

Because you don't want to. But it's true. That's the secret.

VIRGINIA

To believe in nothing?

GEORGE

Not "nothing." Nothing: capital N.

VIRGINIA

Is that Something?

GEORGE

It's Everything. If you believe in Nothing, you can never be disillusioned or disappointed. Nothing can't *not* be enough because—

VIRGINIA

(*Embracing him to stop this*)

Don't talk any more.

GEORGE

You think it's mad, but is it less mad to believe in Man? Or God? Look how insane those sane beliefs have made the world!

VIRGINIA

Please don't talk any more . . .

(*She kisses him.*)

GEORGE

(*Carried away by himself*)

They preach salvation for the world that agrees and destruction for the world that doesn't; love for the fellow-man who says Yea and hate for the fellow-beast who says Nay. (*She sits up and moves away, fixing her hair*) Whatever or whoever your god is, he is the one god, the true god, the only god—(*She yanks the imaginary lamp chain; the light returns*) I've offended you.

VIRGINIA

(*Clicks off the radio*)

How could you offend me with nothing? (*Rising angrily*) The one thing every man wants from a woman is her ears!

GEORGE

Not exactly. But the ears of an intelligent woman—

VIRGINIA

If I were prettier, would you have bothered?

GEORGE

(*Rising*)

Tell a woman she's pretty, she complains you think her dumb. Tell her she's intelligent—(*Shrugs*) Nothing pleases.

VIRGINIA

Which nothing? Yours or something else? Nothing, something, anything, everything: the last words left, and you have made them meaningless. Sense is non-sense. See? I do it, too: verse and reverse, offend and fend off—

GEORGE

I *have* offended you.

VIRGINIA

Yes!

GEORGE

By selling nothing—or by doing nothing?

VIRGINIA

How cruel! By both, if you must know! More by your credo—it's evil! Were you afraid to have me touch your head lest I feel the horns? I'm afraid, you make me afraid, somehow. You frighten me, like everything else in this wood. (*Suddenly*) Are you one of them?

GEORGE

One of whom?

VIRGINIA

They put you up to it. You are a warning of what can happen to me! I can die of nothingness!

GEORGE

What *has* happened to you?

VIRGINIA

Ask me no questions, I know no answers.

GEORGE

A moment ago—

VIRGINIA

A moment ago, I was listening for the secret. Now I know the truth: There is no secret except that you must find the secret for yourself! (*Laughs*) I'll match my hollow circles with yours any day.

GEORGE

No, you'd win hands down. (*Packing up his knapsack*) You didn't like my answer: I disappointed you. (*Turns to her*) Is that how you always react when people don't stand as tall as you've decided they should?

VIRGINIA

React how?

GEORGE

As though you've got to make them even smaller than they are—

VIRGINIA

No!

GEORGE

—Cut them down to pygmies, beetles, ants—

VIRGINIA

No! I did *not* try to cut you down, Andy!

GEORGE

I don't think you could, and the name is still George.

VIRGINIA

George. I meant George.

GEORGE

Well, the charm wore thin a bit ahead of schedule. (*Packing up*) My fault, too: I have a terrible tendency to get fascinated with myself. However—I am full of optimism—(*Straightens up*)—and the woods are full of girls.

VIRGINIA

But they wait for me. Don't leave me alone with them.

GEORGE

What?

VIRGINIA

Please stay.

GEORGE

Why?

VIRGINIA

We could be friends.

GEORGE

That's harder than being lovers.

(*He slings up his knapsack.*)

VIRGINIA

(*Smiles*)

Well, in that case . . . ?

GEORGE

You'd probably be disappointed. You know, I suspect you're always disappointed.

VIRGINIA

Don't be polite. It's you who are disappointed in me.

GEORGE

(Picking up his shotgun)

I suspect you always think that, too.

VIRGINIA

He said that.

GEORGE

Andy?

VIRGINIA

(Pointing to the sweater GINNA *left in the clearing)*

No. They're coming back, he and Ginna. *(*GEORGE *has reached the rim of trees; there is music, and the light goes to strange darkness)* Give me another chance! *(But* GEORGE *steps into the blackness. As he does, from the trees behind* VIRGINIA, *a* YOUNG MAN *steps into the clearing)* Wait!

(Her hand reaches out to GEORGE *just as* GINNA *steps into the clearing, her hand reaching out, in exactly the same way, to the* YOUNG MAN.*)*

GINNA

Please, wait...

(The YOUNG MAN *stops.* VIRGINIA *stops, frozen with fear. Then she tries hard to look around, but cannot turn. Her hand reaches back, fingers extended, as though to shut out and ward off what is behind her. Then, suddenly, she cries out.)*

VIRGINIA

Wait!

(*She runs off into the trees after* GEORGE. *The music stops and* GINNA *and the* YOUNG MAN *unstiffen and move a step. He wears tennis shoes, suntans, a half-buttoned shirt, and picks up the cardigan with the faded letters: "State U." She wears a dressing gown reminiscent—in color? material? cut?—of Virginia's negligee.*)

GINNA

There's no place you can go at this hour, Pete. (*He buttons his shirt*) Come back to the house. (*He rolls down his sleeves*) I'll sleep in Father's study.

PETE

(*Quietly, facing away from her*)

Do you want a divorce?

GINNA

Of course not! (*A step toward him*) Pete, what happened isn't—

PETE

(*Putting on the sweater*)

Ginna, I don't want to talk about it—

GINNA

But you never want to talk about any problem we have. What happened isn't so very terrible. Or even so very unusual.

PETE

Ginna—

GINNA

It happens to most men.

PETE

How often? And afterwards, the politeness of silence in the dark, acting sleep—

GINNA

There is no need to—

PETE

And the excuses for the morning: Gee, I was awfully tired last night; gee, I was awfully drunk last night. When we both know—

GINNA

Don't you know it's humiliating for me, too? (*Now he looks at her*) To know that I don't excite you any more. That you don't find me attractive any more.

PETE

I do. It isn't that.

GINNA

Then, what is it?

PETE

All I know is that I've disappointed you.

GINNA

It's you who are disappointed in me.

PETE

You always think that.

GINNA

You married me because we thought I was going to have a baby—

PETE

We were to be married right after graduation, anyway.

GINNA

We never set a definite date until we thought I was pregnant. Even the doctor thought I was. You'll have to admit that. Even he didn't know it was a false pregnancy and you spoke to him yourself, so—

PETE

What are you doing?!

GINNA

Well—

PETE

Every time you start analyzing, you come up with the wildest—It isn't because I think you trapped me into marriage. Because I never thought that!

GINNA

It never crossed your mind.

PETE

No.

GINNA

But why did you marry me? You were the biggest man on campus: letter man, honor student, council president— (*Proudly*) Remember—the school voted you Man of the Year before you could vote.

PETE

Too bad you can't retire at twenty.

GINNA

(*Unhearing, lost in happy reminiscence*)

I still remember what it felt like to walk into a dance with you, wearing your pin. Or when we met in a corridor, or walked across the campus. I caught your glow and spread it around me in front of all of them. I was somebody, too.

PETE

(*A discovery*)

Is that why you married me?

GINNA

Would that be so wrong?

PETE

Ginna . . . tell me what it feels like to walk into a dance with me now, wearing my ring.

GINNA

You look for the wrong meanings!

PETE

But the biggest man on campus doesn't walk *through* doors now; he can walk right under them—stretched to his full height! His big job now is playing golf with his wife's father!

GINNA

I happen to like my father!

PETE

So do I—

GINNA

I don't mean I want you to become like him—

PETE

Then why did you badger me into quitting the one real job I've had since school?

GINNA

It wasn't good enough for you.

PETE

Apparently the jobs that are good enough, I'm not good enough to get.

GINNA

You are!

PETE

Then why don't I get them?

GINNA

You will!

PETE

When?

GINNA

When you stop swimming laps and doing push-ups and going to games; when you stop being a boy!

PETE

Meaning when I stop living off you.

GINNA

I never said that!

PETE

But it's true and I'm ashamed of it! I'm ashamed of taking from you and not being able to—not standing on my—not being up to what—I'M STRANGLING ON THE DOUBLE MEANINGS!

GINNA

You're analyzing now and being equally—

PETE

And before I said, "Standing stretched to full height," when in my mind it was standing *erect*—

GINNA

Pete, please . . . !

(*Another painful, embarrassed moment.*)

PETE

One thing about jobs. I know you really want more and can do more than this welfare work you—

GINNA

I only want to help you.

PETE

Ginna, I'm drowning! Maybe you think you're helping me to shore, but you can't swim yourself. You keep telling me you fell in love with the biggest man on campus. Well, school's out and the world's in. I'm nothing!

GINNA

That's not so!

PETE

Help me get started to being even a little something.

GINNA

I don't know what to do any more—I've tried, I have—

PETE

But you've given up. Just as you have with—with what I suppose I was really talking about. With making love.

GINNA

I have not! . . . I told you: it's just as bad for me . . . It's no different for a woman.

PETE

Yes, it is. You can fake.

GINNA

Fake?!

PETE

You do. You have.

GINNA

That's crazy!

PETE

I can tell when I hold you in my arms.

GINNA

How like you to blame me!

PETE

And when I fail, I think you're *glad!*
(*Silence.*)

GINNA

(*Angry*)
You can't actually believe that. How dare you even think it!

PETE

I haven't; I just guessed. Ginna, you're glad!

GINNA

You'd better stop that—

PETE

Admit it!

GINNA

No!

PETE

The truth!

GINNA

Truth doesn't exist!

PETE

Skip the fancy evasions. The truth!

GINNA

It isn't!

PETE

Ginna—

GINNA

What's true for you is not true for me!

PETE

Then just what *is* true for you?!

GINNA

(*With a cry*)

I don't know any more: *My heart and mind are strangers!* (*Pause.*)

PETE

I do want a divorce . . . before I do drown.

GINNA

Are you serious?

PETE

Unless there is something you want to say.

GINNA

I am not going to beg, if that's what you mean. I have too much pride for that.

PETE

How can you have pride and still be in love?

GINNA

How can you destroy respect and still ask for love?

PETE

It's pretty silly to stand here and insult one another.

GINNA

Very. So shall we just say good-bye?

PETE

O.K. Good-bye, Ginna.

GINNA

Good-bye. (*They shake hands. He goes into the trees as music is heard. She stands still for a moment, then picks at her gown. Suddenly*) Pete! (*But her voice cracks. The light becomes summer day again. An accent in the music, and* GINNA *alerts, as though she hears someone coming*) Pete?

(*But it is* GEORGE *who enters the clearing. The music goes under.*)

GEORGE

(*The charm*)

Good afternoon. Lovely weather for weather, isn't it?

(VIRGINIA *appears behind him.*)

VIRGINIA

(*Looking coldly at* GINNA)

That depends whether you like weather. (*Smiling at* GEORGE) Personally, I'd rather look out at it than be out in it. (*Takes his arm possessively*) Shall we go inside?

GINNA

(*As they start to the cottage*)

You will, but you shouldn't. (*A step after them*) *I* wouldn't. (*They continue up the steps*) You'll wish you hadn't.

VIRGINIA

(*Whirling around*)

That's not your affair!

GINNA

It won't be yours, either.

VIRGINIA

It will! (*To* GEORGE, *who is on the porch*) She has no idea what she's talking about. She doesn't know the first thing about me—

GINNA

I don't know the last, but I certainly know the first. And the second and the—

VIRGINIA

(*Going toward her*)

You don't really know me at all.

GINNA

Perhaps not.

VIRGINIA

(*To* GEORGE)

You see?

GINNA

But who knows you better?

VIRGINIA

(*Harshly, to* GINNA)

Stop! I will not put up with you any longer. You are to stay away from here and stay away from me.

(*She turns and starts swiftly to the cottage again. But as she reaches the first step she suddenly stops.*)

GEORGE

(*On the porch*)

What is it?

VIRGINIA

(*She holds up her hand. She is listening*)

Don't you hear?

GEORGE

What?

VIRGINIA

Someone is using an ax, someone is chopping wood.

GEORGE

What if someone is?

VIRGINIA

Nothing, I suppose. (*Climbs a step*) But you don't hear it?

GEORGE

No.

GINNA

No, not yet, Virginia. You're jumping time. That comes later, in a little while.

(*But* VIRGINIA *and* GEORGE *have gone into the cottage, shutting the door behind them. A variation of nostalgic music begins. The lighting changes: a slight glow on the cottage door; a deeper, sunnier spread on the grass at the edge of the clearing farthest from the door.* NORA *comes through the trees carrying a thermos and a blanket.*)

NORA

Do you think she'll mind if I have my picnic here?

GINNA

Yes.

NORA

It's such a dreamy spot.

GINNA

She's worse than ever, still pretending she doesn't know who we are.

NORA

Then the hell with her. I'll have it here anyway.

(She begins spreading the blanket in the lighted area.)

GINNA

(Going)

She just won't like us.

NORA

You mean she's not going to take care of us?

GINNA

I doubt it. Unless we force her to.

NORA

That, I'd adore! *(Calling, as* GINNA *goes)* Hazelmae! Hazelmae!

(She lights a cigarette as a girl her own age enters with a small picnic basket. HAZELMAE *has a weight problem and a too thick Southern accent.)*

HAZELMAE

I declare, Nora lamb, over hill over dale to this? It certainly isn't my idea of chic.

(Both girls settle on the blanket during the following, and HAZELMAE *takes a mirror and eyebrow tweezers from the basket and sets to work.)*

NORA

Nature, honey lamb, is not chic.

(She opens the thermos.)

HAZELMAE

The grass is dirty.

NORA

Then so is the sky.

HAZELMAE

I don't know why we didn't go with the rest of the girls, in the first place.

NORA

Because they're children. God, they're so young!

HAZELMAE

It couldn't be because Mistah Pipe-Smoker is in charge of the picnic?

NORA

I am bored with Mistah Pipe-Smoker's love affair with himself. And his hair is too long.

HAZELMAE

You weren't bored until he laughed at your Valentine.

NORA

I knew, I knew, I knew I shouldn't have told you about that.

HAZELMAE

You didn't. I was there.

NORA

Then why make me feel like a fool all over again? (*Hands* HAZELMAE *the cup*) Happiness.

HAZELMAE

What's in it? (*Toasts*) Happiness.

(*She drinks.*)

NORA

Gin and pineapple juice.

HAZELMAE

Not very much gin.

NORA

Then you steal it next time. Your father doesn't drink as much as mine, anyway. (*As the music fades away, the sound of wood-chopping fades in from the trees nearest them*) My father, all fathers! The only time they appear is when we are in danger of enjoying ourselves.

HAZELMAE

My papa calls me honey bucket.

NORA

Is there one single, sane, logical reason why we couldn't have gone to that house party? I ask you!

HAZELMAE

I have blanked it from my mind.

NORA

(*Mimicking*)

"Young ladies don't go to house parties with young gentlemen until they're eighteen." Why? Do they ever tell you why? (*Looking off toward chopping sound*) "Because they just don't, dear." (*Takes out a pair of glasses, the better to see the wood-chopper*) I loathe when they call me dear. He's cute.

(*She puts the glasses away.*)

HAZELMAE

(*Sees where* NORA *is staring*)

Oh. Yeeeeees.

NORA

I saw him first.

HAZELMAE

(*Shrugs*)

All we'll do anyway is talk about him. Simmer down, lamby-pie.

NORA

Simmer yourself down, pie-face. One summer in Nashville three years ago is no excuse for that accent.

HAZELMAE

If you can arbitrarily change your name to Nora, I can certainly change my accent.

NORA

If you just once looked into something besides a mirror—

HAZELMAE

Such as, pray?

NORA

Such as the works of Ibsen, pray—you'd know Nora was the first emancipated woman.

HAZELMAE

Lamb, the purpose of my accent is to make certain that before I am twenty, I am definitely *un*emancipated.

NORA

He's really very cute.

HAZELMAE

Why don't you yell it to him?

NORA

(*Loudly*)

He's really very cute!

(*The cottage door opens and* VIRGINIA *appears, gathering her negligee around her.*)

VIRGINIA

What are you doing?

NORA

Just having a picnic.

VIRGINIA

Must you be so loud?

NORA

Sorry. (VIRGINIA *goes back in*) The hell I am.

HAZELMAE

Cursing and flirting are not qualities for a lady.

NORA

Ladies are not only useless, they're ordinary. I'm not ordinary, nor will I be. The whole beauty of the world is that every single tiny speck in it is different from every other!

HAZELMAE

There you go: doing and saying the opposite just because it is the opposite.

NORA

Cretin! What I do and say is Me! I am Me, I am a Person!

HAZELMAE

Hmmmm . . .

NORA

(*Snatching the mirror*)

Look at you!

HAZELMAE

Smarter than you are. Outside, I save my energy and do as they want. But inside—(*Lies back on the blanket*) I know exactly what I want and I will do it and have it the day I am on my own.

NORA

Too late by then! You'll be stuck in the rut of worrying what *they* think. (*Looking off toward the woodchopper*) That's why nobody lives. *I* worry about what *I* think, and if they don't like it—

(She breaks off. The sound of woodchopping has stopped. She stares off into the trees. HAZELMAE *looks at her, then into the trees, then sits up. From the trees comes a boy of about twenty, wearing faded trousers and a soiled, sweaty singlet. His open, almost wholesome good looks are scarred by the possibility of viciousness in his eyes. He stands and looks at them for a long moment, finally focusing on* NORA.)

THE BOY

Hiyuh.

NORA

Hi.

HAZELMAE

(Weak, scared)

Hi.

THE BOY

(After a moment)

Ya live hereabouts?

NORA

Yes.

THE BOY

Not in the village.

NORA

No.

HAZELMAE

Huh!

THE BOY

I do.

NORA

Oh, but I like the village, it's charming! The atmosphere of these little old—(*He suddenly bursts into laughter*) Well, I happen to think it is charming.

THE BOY

Huffy.

NORA

When I choose to be.

HAZELMAE

(*To* NORA)

I just wouldn't talk to him at all.

THE BOY

Nobody's talking to you, skinny.

NORA

That's mean.

THE BOY

I give back good as I get.

(*He wipes his brow with his forearm.*)

NORA

What's the matter? Hot?

THE BOY

Damn. (*She hands him the thermos. He takes a short drink, frowns, then takes another*) Well! What dya know now! (*Again he laughs—but with a sexual joyousness this time*) What dya know! . . . Got a smoke? (*Takes the cigarette she offers—and waits. She gets matches from* HAZELMAE *and strikes one for him. He inhales slowly and deliberately*) Gonna be here awhile?

NORA

Yes.

THE BOY

(*Stretching*)

Got a murderous job but I'm pretty near through.

(*He goes back into the trees.*)

HAZELMAE

(*Forgetting her Southern accent*)

We're leaving.

NORA

(*Looking off after* THE BOY)

We just got here.

HAZELMAE

Stop showing off.

NORA

I'm not doing a thing.

HAZELMAE

He's filthy and he smells.

(*The woodchopping sound has resumed. The light begins to darken.*)

NORA

Hazelmae, you're a snob.

HAZELMAE

You're not even old enough to go to a house party.

NORA

What makes you old enough? House parties? What *they* say? No, it's everything that's bothering you inside and saying: Do! You're a woman when you *have* to be!

(*The cottage door opens and* VIRGINIA *appears, holding the negligee in front of her.*)

VIRGINIA

(*At a strange high pitch*)

Silly little girl!

NORA

Who says?

VIRGINIA

I can hear you inside, I can hear everything!

NORA

You get so excited.

VIRGINIA

Go on, silly little girl! But not here, get away from here!

HAZELMAE

We're going all right.

(She starts to fold up the blanket as VIRGINIA *goes back inside.)*

NORA

Sometimes I hate her.

HAZELMAE

You're not impressing me one bit. Now come on. *(The wood-chopping sound stops. Frightened)* Nora . . . please come.

NORA

Nothing is going to happen. I can take care of myself.

(She looks at the cottage.)

HAZELMAE

If your father finds out—

NORA

Think I care?

HAZELMAE

Please! Let's hurry before—

(She stops. THE BOY *has returned to the clearing. He wears a shirt now: rolled sleeves, unbuttoned. The cigarette butt is behind one ear. A pause; then he kicks the thermos so that it rolls to* HAZELMAE. *Fearfully, she picks it up. He grins.)*

THE BOY

(*To* NORA)

Running to Momma?

NORA

No . . .

THE BOY

Kids scare easy.

NORA

I'm not a kid.

THE BOY

Boo. (*Coolly, she picks up the picnic basket*) Well?

NORA

Well?

THE BOY

(*Takes the basket and gives it to* HAZELMAE)

Wait up at the road.

HAZELMAE

She's coming with me.

NORA

We *are* together . . .

THE BOY

(*To* HAZELMAE)

Wait up at the road, kid.

HAZELMAE

Nora—

THE BOY

The baby's afraid of the woods.

NORA

Don't hang on me, Hazelmae. I'll be along in a minute.

(HAZELMAE *hesitates, but* THE BOY *gestures with his head for her to go. She looks at him, at* NORA, *then runs quickly from the clearing.* NORA *smiles,* THE BOY *doesn't.*)

NORA

It's very pretty here, isn't it?

THE BOY

It's pretty.

NORA

In summer, everything is so tender. Except the colors. I mean . . .

THE BOY

The colors're soft in the shade . . .

NORA

Hazelmae and I always . . .

THE BOY

Like deep under the trees . . .

NORA

I've tried painting . . .

THE BOY

Come on.

NORA

Where?

THE BOY

You been here before.

NORA

Yes, but . . .

THE BOY

You're not just all big talk?

NORA

No.

THE BOY

Then come on.

NORA

I . . . I should really . . .

THE BOY

Come on.

(He takes her arm to turn her around, then gives her a little push ahead of him. She walks slowly into the trees. He takes the cigarette stub from behind his ear, puts it in his pocket and follows her.

The light in the clearing is black and white now. A moment; then, to the rising wail of a clarinet, VIRGINIA *comes running out of the cottage, wearing a dress not completely fastened. She tears down the steps, across the clearing, hands outstretched, mouth open, until she reaches the spot where* NORA *and* THE BOY *disappeared. Instead of a scream, however, there is the shriek of the clarinet. Then blank silence.*

She stands dead still a moment; then abruptly, violently, turns, cradling her hunched body. A low moan escapes her. GEORGE *comes out on the porch, his shirttails flapping loose. She darts into a black shadow.*)

VIRGINIA

Don't come out like that!

GEORGE

(*Buttoning the shirt*)

There's no one here.

VIRGINIA

There is, there is! (*He starts down into the clearing*) Stay away!

GEORGE

(*Walks into a black shadow. Then*)

Are you that sorry? (*No answer*) Why do what you don't enjoy?

VIRGINIA

I thought I would . . . I wanted to. (*His clothes in order, he appears in light as he goes to the porch for his knapsack. She moves into light as she steps toward him*) I couldn't: I kept hearing her, them.

GEORGE

Hearing who?

VIRGINIA

They are opening old closets and bringing out dirty clothes I'm not sure are mine. And they do it deliberately! Yes! They want to drive me into ways I hate! They do, Andy!

GEORGE

(*Sharply*)

I'm not Andy.

VIRGINIA

(*Looking back at the trees*)

No. I'm sorry.

GEORGE

Who is this Andy?

VIRGINIA

No one important.

GEORGE

But you keep calling him. Why?

VIRGINIA

Why must you know? I don't remember!

GINNA

(*Stepping from the trees into light;* GEORGE *steps into blackness*)

I think she's afraid to remember.

VIRGINIA

I'm not!

GINNA

If you weren't, you might stop calling (*Mimicking*) Andy, Andy—

VIRGINIA

You make too much of him. He's only another I don't want to remember. The woods are full of them!

GINNA

Full of memories?

VIRGINIA

No! George, stop her, make her—(*But* GEORGE *is gone*) You drove him away.

GINNA

You never really wanted him. You were even wishing he would disintegrate afterwards, weren't you?

VIRGINIA

All right. Yes.

GINNA

Then, I did you a favor.

VIRGINIA

But you pushed me to him!

GINNA

What?!

VIRGINIA

By telling me not to do it. You *do* know me, you know that's all I need to make me go ahead. I wouldn't have if it weren't for you! I wouldn't have finally hurt my father if it weren't for Jigee! You drive me into doing things, all three of you! Deliberately! Is that your method of winning me over to like you? Interfering, driving me to do what I don't want, driving me to remember what I hate? Why must you keep bringing back and bringing back and bringing back—(JIGEE *steps into the light in the clearing from another part of the woods. She holds the garden shears in front of her.* VIRGINIA *stares at them. Then*) I didn't want to hurt you, Daddy. I wanted to make you *see* me. I wanted—(*Stops. Looks around for* BARNEY, *then at the girls*) *Someone help!* (*Silence. Then*) Don't come any nearer. You lied when you said you welcome me home. This nightmare imitation is not home. You lie when you say you want me to take care of you. You want something terrible to happen to me. I do *not* know who you are, but I know you are evil! I will not let anything more happen. You are getting out of here at once, immediately! I'm not asking you now, I'm telling you, ordering you: go away and stay away. (*The girls do not move*) Very well. I shall get my father to help.

JIGEE

Him!

GINNA

What makes you suddenly think he'll help?

VIRGINIA

He loves me.

GINNA

You *are* a fool. (VIRGINIA *moves, but so does* GINNA) What can he do now, anyway? It's you and us.

VIRGINIA

No.

GINNA

It always has been.

VIRGINIA

No!

(*She turns and starts to the trees in the direction of the house.* GINNA *blocks her way.* VIRGINIA *looks at her, then turns and starts out at another angle. This time* JIGEE *moves to block her—with the shears held straight out.* VIRGINIA *looks from one to the other, then whirls and half runs across the clearing. Just as she reaches the edge,* NORA *steps into light, blocking her way.*

A hollow, reverberating sound begins; like an oscillating heartbeat. Faint at first, louder and louder until the curtain.

Slowly, VIRGINIA *backs away from* NORA. *The clearing is quite dark now. She is in a pool of light, the three girls in a half-shadowed semicircle around her.*)

VIRGINIA

You can't do this. You have no right to be here. I live here. This is my home.

GINNA

Your home?

VIRGINIA

Yes! Who do you think you are?

GINNA

Who do you think we are?

VIRGINIA

This is my home. I belong here. I live here.

NORA

(*A mimicking echo*)

I live here.

JIGEE

(*Also mimicking*)

I live here.

GINNA

(*Hurling it at* VIRGINIA)

I live here!

VIRGINIA

I *do!*

JIGEE

(*Mimicking*)

I do.

GINNA

(*Mimicking*)

I do.

NORA

I do!

VIRGINIA

I do! I am Virginia!

GINNA

I am Virginia!

NORA

I am Virginia!

JIGEE

I am Virginia!

VIRGINIA

I am!

THE GIRLS

(*Overlapping*)

I am! *I* am! *I* am! *I* am! *I* am! *I* am! *I* am!

(*Their shouting drowns out* VIRGINIA. *Music has begun. She turns from one to another in panic as they and the light close in on her and the oscillating beat is louder, heavier, punctuating their cries. Her hands go to her ears and at last she screams—and blindly tears through them up the steps to the cottage as*

The Curtain Falls

ACT TWO

ACT TWO

In the darkness, music and the oscillating heartbeat sound. As the lights come up, the music softens to fade away. The cottage is moved further onstage, projecting into the clearing, which is a web of shadows. One room is visible which has two doors: one leading to the porch, one to an unseen hall. There is a window in the third wall. Little furniture: a chair, a bed, a chest. A Japanese lantern sags from the ceiling; an old typewriter is half under the bed; a crippled doll droops on the floor. Clothes spill out of the chest: some of them have the shape and color of dresses the three girls wore. VIRGINIA's *negligee is on the chair.*

As the scene opens, VIRGINIA *is running into the room. She slams the porch door shut, locks it, locks the hall door, closes the window shutters. Her breathing is heavy, desperate.*

VIRGINIA

One and one is two. Two times two is four. Four times four is sixteen. (*Her breathing is getting calmer. The sound of the heartbeat is fainter. She lies on the bed*) Sixteen times sixteen . . . Six times six is thirty-six. Six, carry three. Six times one is six . . . and three is nine. (*In control now, she takes a deep, shuddering breath, gets up and starts to smooth her dress. The heartbeat sound stops. She takes the dress off—she is wearing a slip—and lays it neatly on the bed. Going to the porch door, she hesitates, then unlocks it—and throws it wide open. Only stillness outside. As she goes back to put on her negligee, a shadow seems to move in the clearing. Unaware, she unlocks the hall door. She has turned away when the door opens and* GINNA *enters the room.* VIRGINIA *stops in the middle of fastening her robe. A look at* GINNA, *then she turns away as though the girl were not there. But as she faces toward the porch,* NORA *enters from that door. A moment. Then, deliberately fastening, fixing, tying the negligee, she turns so that she is not facing either girl, and begins again*) Sixteen times sixteen. Six times six is thirty-six.

GINNA

The connection between arithmetic and a sound mind never did add up.

NORA

She's not adding, she's multiplying.

GINNA

Fear times fright equals madness.

NORA

Carry confusion.

VIRGINIA

(*Continuing to mumble through their conversation*)

Carry three. Six times one is six and three is—is nine. Ninety-sick . . . *six!*

(*She gasps on the last word as the shutters crack back.* JIGEE *peers in.*)

JIGEE

Sick sick sick. She's madly sick!

(*She starts clambering in.*)

VIRGINIA

(*Desperately*)

Six, ninety-six. And sixteen. No, and a hundred and sixty—

NORA

(*Conversationally, to* GINNA)

Times two? Oh, my dear, three to the eighth degree!

GINNA

I know a wonderful πr squared who will divide nine for next to zero!

(VIRGINIA *has seated herself in the chair, her hands over her ears, eyes closed. She rocks back and forth, trying to complete her multiplication.*)

NORA

Better than seven hypotenuse?

GINNA

Rhomboid twelve!

NORA

Ten!

GINNA

Four!

JIGEE

Bingo! (*Pointing to* VIRGINIA) What's she doing?

GINNA

Trying to ignore that we're here.

JIGEE

Oh, then where are we?

NORA

In her head.

JIGEE

Very sick indeed. (*Going very close to* VIRGINIA) You don't think I'm in your head, do you? (*Moves to the other side as* VIRGINIA *turns away*) If you don't answer, that means you do think so.

NORA

(*Coming to the other side of* VIRGINIA)

And if you do think so, you *are* crazy. (VIRGINIA *hunches up*) See?

JIGEE

She is crazy! Is is is! Cuckoo! You're her and Ginna's her and I'm her; we're all her, and I love it!

(*On this, she zips off her hat and grabs one from the chest. It is much too big.*)

GINNA

Jigee!

JIGEE

I'm sick of my old one, and as long as I'm her, it's mine anyway!

NORA

In that case—

(She snatches a robe from the chest.)

GINNA

Well, I've always liked this. (*Puts on a cape*) Are there gloves to match?

JIGEE

You're her: you ought to know.

(Laughs madly. All three rummage wildly through VIRGINIA'S *clothes, while she darts to a corner, then watches them, fury building inside her. The heartbeat sound builds with her fury.)*

NORA

Oh, this fits perfectly!

GINNA

You look sweet in it.

NORA

We look sweet in it. But it just demands that hat.

(She snatches the one JIGEE *wears.)*

JIGEE

That's mine!

NORA

It's hers.

GINNA

Girls—

JIGEE

Well, I'm her.

NORA

So am I.

JIGEE

But I was her first and I took it first.

NORA

Jigee, as long as I'm her and you're her, then it follows you're me and I'm you. Therefore, *I* took it first and it's mine, thank you very much.

JIGEE

Something's very wrong. (*Rummaging again*) Oh, well, I'll take—

(*But* VIRGINIA *is suddenly on her like a fury. The heart-beat sound stops.*)

VIRGINIA

(*Throwing clothes*)

Take this and this and this! (*A long party dress*) It's light as a memory, a dream for dancing. And it fits perfectly because you're me. Oh, it might be a bit long, but you can take it in here and hold it in here and tuck it in here—(*Grabbing the hat from* NORA) And it just demands this hat, doesn't it? (*Grabbing cape from* GINNA) And this to make you look sweet. (*Grabbing more clothes*) And this and this—YOU KNOW WHO YOU ARE! What's Ginna but a nickname for Virginia? (*To* NORA) What were you called before you called yourself Nora? (*To* JIGEE) And before that, because you couldn't pronounce Virginia, because you twisted it, why do you all twist me now? You are *not* me! I *have* been sick—I have been driven half-mad by a team of three white nightmares! That's all you are. You aren't me. You aren't here. You *aren't even real!* (*Turns away from them. Quietly*) *They* aren't real. They don't even exist.

GINNA

(*After a frozen moment*)

No?

(*She pushes a chair over. It crashes.*)

NORA

(*Holding out her hand*)

Touch.

JIGEE

Feel.

(*She touches* VIRGINIA, *who, with a cry, darts out to the porch.*)

GINNA

We exist—as long as you exist.

(GINNA *comes out on the porch.*)

VIRGINIA

What is it you want?

GINNA

(*Cold*)

You've known from the beginning.

NORA

(*Coming out on the porch*)

We told you straight off.

VIRGINIA

You want me to take care of you.

JIGEE

(*Coming out on the porch*)

Yes.

VIRGINIA

To like you.

NORA

Yes.

VIRGINIA

Why?!

GINNA

Because we belong to you as you belong to us.

VIRGINIA

I belong to no one! (*She runs down into the clearing*) I will be held down by no one! I *don't* like you. You're weak, defiant, destructive, *unloved!* You have settled for the second rate because that's what *you* are!

GINNA

(*Caustically*)

We're willing to settle for you.

VIRGINIA

I will not be settled for! Nor will I settle! I have never accepted what is less than I want and I will not accept you!

NORA

Then fight us. But watch out.

JIGEE

Watch what we can really do.

VIRGINIA

You can make me do nothing—because without me you are nothing!

GINNA

You are nothing without us.

VIRGINIA

With you, I am nothing, *with* you. Yes. Yes! (*Slowly*) *It is because of you I have been nothing.* (*Claps her hands in glee*) Of course! Three miseries have goaded me into confusion and madness and stupidity, into attempting to settle as you have, into being a mirror of you! (*Laughs*) Misery loves company—but thank you, no. Thank you for the offer, dear ladies; thank you for the enlightenment, dear fools! But no! We are going to part company—*now!*

(*She thrusts out her hands: music begins and the light changes. The girls stand transfixed, then their bodies begin to sway. The cottage begins to move back to its original position, to music.*)

JIGEE

No . . .

NORA

We can't be divided this way.

GINNA

We're inseparable.

VIRGINIA

(*Pushing outward with her upraised hands as though against an almost immovable force*)

I put you out of mind—now—and—*forever!*

(*Slowly, as though vainly resisting an enormous pull, the girls start back into the blackness. They speak with great difficulty now.*)

NORA

You can't—get—rid of us!

GINNA

You can't—get—free—of—us!

JIGEE

You—can't.

VIRGINIA

(Pushing harder, but exulting)

I can—I will—I am—

GINNA

(Her voice fading as she fades from sight)

There's a way . . . but not—like—this . . .

NORA

(Fading into the blackness)

Not—like—this—Virginia . . .

JIGEE

(Going off)

Not—like—this . . .

(A surge of music; bright sunlight pours down on the clearing and on the cottage porch; the girls are gone! VIRGINIA *whirls joyously.)*

VIRGINIA

(Crying out)

Hello! *(Almost dancing about the clearing and up the porch steps)* Hello, morning! Hello, sunlight! Hello, home! Hello—*Me! (The music is gay and sweet, the lights are warm pink)*

Now I can be! Whom shall I be, what shall I have? Order and neatness—and pleasure from the familiar . . . Expectation and delight—and the excitement of caring. And—yes! I can be *right!* . . . And descending into the world again, I can like what I wear, and where I live. I have changed so I can change things as they were—(*The music stops*)—into things as they will be! No more aloneness! I can even have—(*A stronger light has been glowing at the opposite edge of the trees. On the porch now, she alerts; then, softly*) Andy? (*Leaning across the rail*) Andy? (*She seems to see something coming through the trees, for, happily, she runs across to the light glow, calling*) *ANDY!* (*Just before she reaches it, a man steps out of the trees and she stops. Older than she, he is personable, dressed casually. He has a quiet assurance and an ease—and a strength not to be tested. He is* ANDY) . . . Are you really here?

ANDY

(*Smiling*)

I seemed to hear you calling—

VIRGINIA

I was!

ANDY

So I got into my very splendid car—

VIRGINIA

You still haven't traded it in!—

ANDY

Still haven't found time.

VIRGINIA

And does it still break down the way it did on our lovely week-ends?

ANDY

No, that I fixed. It brought me here in no time. (*Looking around*) It's very pretty, but exactly where are we?

VIRGINIA

Two years from yesterday!

ANDY

Doesn't your father live—

VIRGINIA

Careful! (*He stops. She takes his hand and leads him*) You enter this way. Lift!

(*They lift their legs as though they are climbing over an invisible obstacle. There is the "magic circle" music, as earlier.*)

ANDY

Magic circle?

VIRGINIA

Since childhood. It's bewitched in the very nicest way.

ANDY

How is that?

VIRGINIA

What can't you remember?

ANDY

Test me.

VIRGINIA

The last time we were together.

ANDY

The day we were all set to go downtown for our marriage license—

VIRGINIA

The rainy day we never did go, the terrible day of those ugly words—

(*She stops. He looks at her gently, then smiles.*)

ANDY

Spit three times, cross your eyes and look over your left shoulder at the moon in the mirror.

VIRGINIA

There is no moon and I have no mirror.

ANDY

A kiss will do. (*She kisses him. He smiles*) I'm bewitched.

That day never happened, the words were never said. I remember only up to that day. That's where we are, isn't it?

VIRGINIA

No! We're here, it's now! We've just dropped that day out of the world.

ANDY

It had better be a very strong magic circle.

VIRGINIA

Oh, it is!

ANDY

Then we must hurry. We're late.

VIRGINIA

For what?

ANDY

Our wedding. Two years late.

VIRGINIA

(*Happily*)

But not too late, are we?

ANDY

No. Right on time!

VIRGINIA

Better than before!

ANDY

Much! Come on, get your coat.

VIRGINIA

Coat?

ANDY

Hurry. I have to get back to the lab.

VIRGINIA

Last time we hurried; not now. It's not raining. It's a clean new day and I'm a new girl. That's quite apparent, isn't it?

ANDY

Some change is apparent, but you'd better tell me just where.

VIRGINIA

Inside. I've driven them out.

ANDY

Who?

VIRGINIA

The phantoms who have been driving me. I've been cleaning out memories: they're banished! Moved out, so we can move— Yes! We're moving. I have lovely news!

ANDY

You found us an apartment.

VIRGINIA

It's enormous. Well, big.

ANDY

How big?

VIRGINIA

I signed the lease. I had to, Andy, the man said—

ANDY

(*Laughs*)

All right.

VIRGINIA

I'm going to give away all that spindly French furniture of mine—we'll use yours and get more like it—and, oh, there is one whole room for you!

ANDY

One whole small room.

VIRGINIA

It has a view of the river and the city—

ANDY

Still small—

VIRGINIA

There's more than enough space for your books and your records—

ANDY

And those paintings you don't like—

VIRGINIA

Don't understand—

ANDY

Same thing.

VIRGINIA

Well—yes.

ANDY

(*Laughs*)

You were so surprised the first time you saw my place.

VIRGINIA

Well, it's so handsome.

ANDY

What did you expect? Antiseptic modern.

VIRGINIA

No. Filing cabinets with an unpainted door across them for a desk, and lots of test tubes and microscopes and burners. And the missing back seat of your car for the bed.

ANDY

(*They laugh and kiss*)

I really have to get back to the store.

VIRGINIA

Why does kissing me always remind you of work?

ANDY

It reminded me of that license. Come on.

VIRGINIA

Shall we take my car?

ANDY

No.

VIRGINIA

But—

ANDY

No.

VIRGINIA

All right, we're off!

ANDY

What about your coat?

VIRGINIA

Do you feel one drop of rain?

ANDY

No.

VIRGINIA

You see? It's not that other day.

ANDY

O.K. It's a new day, you're a new girl, but I'm the same old workhorse—

VIRGINIA

No.

ANDY

And I still have to get back to the hospital.

VIRGINIA

They can wait.

ANDY

For me?

VIRGINIA

You're a new man. Yes, that's it. You're a very important man now! You got the new appointment!

(*A tremor of music.*)

ANDY

Virginia—

VIRGINIA

You did!

ANDY

I didn't and you know it. I told you—

VIRGINIA

But that day never happened. We just agreed to lose that day.

ANDY

Virginia, be careful. You're going to lose everything.

VIRGINIA

So you might still get the appointment!

GINNA'S VOICE

(From the trees)

He won't and you know it.

VIRGINIA

You will get it!

ANDY

Why is it so terribly important to you? What are you afraid of?

VIRGINIA

The secret in the willow tree; the meaning of the moon.

ANDY

(Grabbing her)

Virginia, what's frightening you?

VIRGINIA

It's never suddenly clear and wonderful: the telegram never comes. I can't keep us in the circle!

ANDY

Must we stay there?

VIRGINIA

Yes. Please.

ANDY

All right. Lead me back. (*She takes his hand and they again step up and over into the circle, to music*) Here I am again.

VIRGINIA

(*Lightly*)

And you're late. I've been calling you.

ANDY

Your father came by the hospital just as I was leaving. No, purely a social call.

VIRGINIA

On you?!

ANDY

Yes. That one lunch the three of us had years ago wasn't much of an opportunity to talk, so I dropped him a note last fall and asked him—

VIRGINIA

(*Sharply*)

Why didn't he tell me?

ANDY

Perhaps he did and you forgot.

VIRGINIA

Anyway, I'm glad you saw him. Barney's fun, isn't he? And much deeper than he seems at first. He's so busy raking leaves over what he feels that—well, for one thing, you'd never guess how deeply he loves me.

ANDY

Virginia, don't let him hurt you.

VIRGINIA

He doesn't. And he wouldn't!

ANDY

Your father is amusing, and easy to get on with so long as—

VIRGINIA

I almost forgot to tell you: I have wonderful news!

ANDY

Virginia—

VIRGINIA

I found us an apartment! Finally! And it's enormous!

ANDY

Not too enormous, I hope.

VIRGINIA

Why? You said—

ANDY

I didn't get the appointment.

VIRGINIA

Oh . . . (*A tremor of music*) It really isn't such a big apartment. You know how I exaggerate. We can certainly manage if I keep my job—

ANDY

But you wanted to give it up.

VIRGINIA

I'll give it up next year—or the year after.

ANDY

I'm sorry. I know it's disappointing to—

VIRGINIA

If we're going to get that license—

ANDY

Virginia—

VIRGINIA

It's late and you have to be back, don't you?

ANDY

Yes.

VIRGINIA

Your car or mine?

ANDY

Mine's outside.

VIRGINIA

Then let's be on our way—

ANDY

Downtown.

(*Music begins to build.*)

VIRGINIA

Andy!

ANDY

That's where the license bureau is.

VIRGINIA

Yes . . .

(*She turns toward cottage.*)

ANDY

It looks like rain.

VIRGINIA

(*Going to the cottage*)

Yes.

ANDY

You'd better take a coat.

VIRGINIA

Yes.

(GINNA *laughs in the trees; then* NORA.)

ANDY

What is it?

VIRGINIA

(*Walking slowly, without turning*)

Nothing.

GINNA'S VOICE

Liar.

ANDY

The appointment meant a good deal to you, didn't it?

VIRGINIA

No.

NORA'S VOICE

Liar.

ANDY

You're very disappointed.

VIRGINIA

No.

JIGEE'S VOICE

Liar.

VIRGINIA

(Whirling around)

I'm not lying! I'm not disappointed!

(Music stops.)

ANDY

No, you're angry!

VIRGINIA

Yes, I'm angry. I'm angry because—

GINNA'S VOICE

He's a failure!

VIRGINIA

Because politics are always involved in these appointments. It's not fair, and I'm angry for you!

ANDY

It was perfectly fair and there were no politics.

VIRGINIA

Then—why didn't you get it?

ANDY

The other man was better.

GINNA'S VOICE

How noble!

VIRGINIA

Stop it!

ANDY

I don't take pleasure in admitting that.

VIRGINIA

Then why do you?

ANDY

Because he is better.

VIRGINIA

He isn't! He couldn't be!

ANDY

Look—

VIRGINIA

I know you: you're brilliant, you've a wonderful mind and a wonderful talent, and you work so hard—you are the best!

ANDY

Virginia, I am not the best . . . I'm good; I'm working hard to be better. And I think I will be. But that fantasy of yours of a near-genius—Virginia, that I am not, nor will I ever be.

GINNA'S VOICE

Translation: mediocre.

NORA'S VOICE

Everyday.

JIGEE'S VOICE

Ordinary.

VIRGINIA

No . . .

ANDY

I'll never be the best, either. But there are other appointments—

GINNA'S VOICE

He'll never get them.

NORA'S VOICE

He's given up—

JIGEE'S VOICE

Settled—

NORA'S VOICE

Quit!

GINNA'S VOICE

He should: he's ordinary!

ANDY

Virginia—

VIRGINIA

I won't let you be ordinary! I mean—you're not, and you haven't given up, have you?

ANDY

Given up what?

VIRGINIA

You haven't settled for being less than you can be and should be? You haven't stopped trying?

ANDY

No.

GINNA'S VOICE

No, he's just no good.

VIRGINIA

You *are* good! You didn't try!

ANDY

Now, wait—

VIRGINIA

I know there's a comfort in settling—

NORA'S VOICE

You settled for him—

VIRGINIA

A relief in sitting with the spectators—

GINNA'S VOICE

How do you like your seat?

VIRGINIA

A safeness in saying, All right, I'm ordinary—

ANDY

That's about enough! . . . Now I am not ordinary. Nor have I settled for anything but the knowledge of what my limitations are. I'm old enough to accept them and that makes life a helluva lot happier. People who don't, Virginia, those people draw and quarter themselves. And if they keep at it too long, there is no thread strong enough to stitch them back together . . . I tried for that appointment—hard. I always try—and you know that, don't you?

VIRGINIA

Yes.

ANDY

Then you can't be angry with me for not trying.

VIRGINIA

No.

ANDY

But you are angry.

VIRGINIA

I—

ANDY

Why?

VIRGINIA

I don't know.

ANDY

There can only be one other reason. You're angry at me because I failed. (*From each side come the voices of the three girls, in turn: "True! True! True!"*) Well?

VIRGINIA

The circle—!

ANDY

There is no magic.

VIRGINIA

Help me back—!

ANDY

We are back.

VIRGINIA

Andy—

ANDY

Say it: you're angry because I failed!

VIRGINIA

Yes! I am! It's true!

(*A pause.*)

ANDY

Why didn't you tell me how important it is to you that I succeed?

VIRGINIA

I was afraid. I was afraid if you knew, you'd stop loving me.

ANDY

Why?!

VIRGINIA

It doesn't mat—

ANDY

Why?

VIRGINIA

Because you'd know me. I'd give myself away and you'd realize I was not what you thought. And I'm not! To care so much about—well, success. And your car—I *am* ashamed being seen in it. I've lied to my friends about your real position—I invent awards and prizes—

ANDY

You're talking like a child, like a bad little girl who—

VIRGINIA

Don't say that to me! *Don't you ever say that to me!*

ANDY

But you are talking like a child! No, you listen! I am obviously less, much less than you thought. That's clear now. You thought I was so brilliant, I'd walk away with that appointment and probably the whole laboratory *and* the hospital. All right. You know otherwise now, Virginia, but that hasn't made you stop—

(*He stops. A pause.*)

VIRGINIA

It hasn't. I swear it hasn't.

ANDY

The idiots we can be, the arrogant idiots. I love you as you are, so of course you love me as I am. We take others for granted when we ourselves can be taken for granted.

VIRGINIA

I do love you!

ANDY

But you know me now. And you said if I knew you, I couldn't love you. No, look at me. LOOK AT ME! . . . Don't you know that *loving is knowing someone and still loving?*

VIRGINIA

No!

ANDY

No, for you, it's the opposite, isn't it? For you, the man who knows you and still loves you can only be ordinary. And an ordinary human being isn't worth your love, so you're protected! You're safe from the pain of ever loving! How neat and—clean —and—disgusting! . . . You know how long you loved me? Exactly as long as you loved that ex-husband I was fool enough to be jealous of: NOT ONE MINUTE! You loved a dream he never was, and a dream I never was! But a real person—that you've *never* loved, have you? A real, live human being with four heads and black thoughts and weaknesses and flaws and *failures*—have you? Can you? There's a point: *can* you love? Can you even feel? Right now, right this instant, standing right here—*do you feel anything?*

VIRGINIA

(*Savagely*)

Yes! *Hatred—of me! I am the enemy!* I hate that I demand you be extraordinary, and yet I demand it! I hate that I demand *I* be, and yet I demand it! I hate that because you are not, I don't love you. But I don't, I can't! And if I cannot love you—*You*— The riddle is unriddled! The joker is pulled out and the card house falls in! I cannot love you because I—*cannot—love—any-one!* The truth came out of your anger; how do you like the sound of it? *I cannot love!*

ANDY

Virginia—

VIRGINIA

They are Virginia, not I. I am no one! How can you *be* when you don't have even the hope of loving!

ANDY

Wait. You're in trouble now, but it's nothing that can't be—

VIRGINIA

Then, even my trouble is ordinary, and I hate that! It's as common as a cold, but how do you cure it? How do you end it? How do I end it? How do I stop me from doing what I am doing right this minute? I—*destroy!* (*Pause*) Loving is knowing someone and still loving? Very well, you know me now. Now *you* look at *me.*

(*For a brief instant, she looks up at his pained face. There is scarcely any light except that on them. She turns away just as he speaks, but at the same moment there is music and she does not hear him.*)

ANDY

I love you.

VIRGINIA

(*Bitterly*)

How very clear is the answer.

ANDY

(*As the light on him fades him out, and his voice with it*)
No! Virginia, you're not hearing. I love you; let me try to help you—

(*But what* VIRGINIA *hears instead is* GINNA *who appears in a light on the cottage porch.*)

GINNA

And you can't like us.

(*As* ANDY *disappears into blackness, light comes up on the porch. The music stops as* GINNA *joins* JIGEE *and* NORA *who are playing cards.*)

NORA

She certainly got rid of us, didn't she?

JIGEE

We sure got rid of him, though.

GINNA

We did her a favor. He isn't what she really wants.

JIGEE

He's common as dirt.

NORA

You could plant flowers in him. (JIGEE *falls over the cards, laughing*) Don't cheat.

JIGEE

You do.

NORA

I'm older.

GINNA

Poor Virginia.

JIGEE

Can't she play?

GINNA

She can't love.

NORA

Especially not us.

(*They all laugh.*)

VIRGINIA

Laugh. Nothing destroys like laughter. Nothing hurts like laughter. Nothing is as safe as laughter.

JIGEE

That's my card!

VIRGINIA

Go on, laugh! You're only laughing at yourselves.

GINNA

If laughter destroys—wait your turn, Jigee—why doesn't she laugh at us?

NORA

She'd rather kill in an uglier way. Gas, for example.

JIGEE

She's got enough clothes to stuff under the doors.

GINNA

The stove might explode.

NORA

She could push us off the cliff into the sea.

JIGEE

No! The rocks would hurt.

GINNA

Hanging!

NORA

I tried that once at school.

JIGEE

Why?

NORA

I forget now.

GINNA

Anyway, she didn't kick the chair out from under her until she heard little ole Hazelmae open the door.

NORA

Everyone was brilliant to me for a whole week after.

(*In the trees near* VIRGINIA *a single bulb begins to glow very slowly.*)

JIGEE

Why doesn't she cut our wrists? Drip drip drip.

GINNA

Poison's neater.

NORA

Where do you get it?

GINNA

Sleeping pills.

(*Faintly, the oscillating heartbeat sound begins.*)

NORA

Dreamy! Does she have any?

JIGEE

In the bathroom medicine chest. I looked.

(VIRGINIA *backs away from the bulb as, during the following,* GINNA *goes to it and pantomimes opening the chest, taking out a bottle and dumping pills into her palm.*)

NORA

Does she have enough for all three of us?

JIGEE

She's got tons. (*Going outside*) And such pretty colors.

NORA

I hope there are enough for three.

GINNA

No.

NORA

What a shame!

JIGEE

Are you positive?

GINNA

Enough for one, though. Who shall it be, Virginia?

NORA

Which of us do you loathe most?

JIGEE

(*Jumping up and down*)

I know, I know!

NORA

If you say me—

JIGEE

I know how she can get rid of all three of us at once! With only those pills!

NORA

Yes!

GINNA

Of course!

(*She thrusts the pills out to* VIRGINIA.)

JIGEE

It was my idea.

GINNA

Yes, it was and I'm sure Virginia will give you full credit. Virginia?

(*A sound escapes from* VIRGINIA *as she backs away from the outstretched hand.*)

JIGEE

Why not?

GINNA

It's such a pleasant way.

NORA

And quiet.

(VIRGINIA *shakes her head.*)

GINNA

Now, Virginia. Are you happy?

JIGEE

No.

GINNA

Have you anything to live for?

NORA

No.

GINNA

Is there anyone you'd hurt if you took these? Anyone who'd care?

NORA

Think hard.

GINNA

There might be someone.

JIGEE

Barney?

NORA

He cares less than a stranger. George?

GINNA

The Georges only care about themselves.

JIGEE

Andy?

NORA

He might care.

GINNA

At least, he'd see she was sorry for what she did.

JIGEE

And he'd be sorry.

GINNA

That's not good enough. Isn't there someone, anyone who really cares?

JIGEE

. . . Us.

NORA

She doesn't care whether we care or not.

GINNA

Then take the pills! (*She puts them into* VIRGINIA's *hand. The oscillating sound gets louder and accelerates*) Quickly now. Don't hesitate.

NORA

It won't hurt.

JIGEE

It's the best way.

GINNA

The easiest. And there's nobody to care.

NORA

Not a soul.

JIGEE

No one.

(*Now* VIRGINIA'S *breathing is in the same tempo as the sound: fast, loud, frightening. She stares at the pills, brings them closer, closer to her mouth, opens her mouth —and the sound suspends. A fraction of a second—and she opens her hand, flinging the pills away.*

Immediately, a crashing rush of music; the lights flicker; a whirl of color coupled with the projection of falling shadows. The three girls break away from VIRGINIA *and run wildly across the clearing. Other figures seem to come from the trees, meet them, turn, cross, dart back again into the shadows and the trees.*

The effect should be that of the moment in space between window ledge and street, between awareness and sliding into a faint: a confusion of color, sound, people, thoughts: jagged, whirling, swift. And through it all, VIRGINIA, *lost, flailing the air with her arms, trying to climb back to safety, to air, until at last she cries out.*)

VIRGINIA

No! There is someone! (*Music and sound stop. The girls stop, turn, look at her. A light slices down on her and begins to spread its glow*) There's *me: I care!* (*The tension in the girls' bodies relaxes. The clearing is still; the light is pleasant as it spreads out. And the music that sounds is a gentle beginning to a resolution of the nostalgic theme. Proudly*) *I* care.

(*The music is sweet; a shudder runs through* VIRGINIA, *then her breathing subsides and becomes gentle, easy. She sits down and* GINNA *slowly walks to her.*)

GINNA

(*With great tenderness*)

I'm glad.

JIGEE

(*Joining them*)

I am, too.

VIRGINIA

Glad?

GINNA

Yes.

VIRGINIA

Why?

NORA

(*As the music dies*)

They think now you can begin to care about us.

JIGEE

She can! (*To* VIRGINIA) And you want to, don't you?

VIRGINIA

(*Surprised herself*)

Yes. I do now!

NORA

You may want to, but you won't.

GINNA

Nora—!

NORA

Look at the dazzling marvels you want us to be—and look at what we are. You know us.

VIRGINIA

I don't. I know only the dark side, and there must be another. Show it to me; help me to see it; make me see it! I really want to like you. Help me.

JIGEE

How?

(*A moment.*)

GINNA

Well, we might . . .

NORA

Might what?

GINNA

Has anyone ever liked us? Not a vague friend or quick lover.

Someone who really knew us. (*To* VIRGINIA) That would help, wouldn't it?

VIRGINIA

Yes!

NORA

(*Bitterly*)

Well, Ginna? Has anyone ever liked you?

GINNA

(*Hesitates, then to* JIGEE)

Has anyone ever liked you?

JIGEE

(*Defiantly, to* NORA)

Has anyone ever liked you?

(*Pause.*)

VIRGINIA

But there must be someone!

NORA

(*Caustically*)

A witness—to prove we're worth being liked despite what we are.

VIRGINIA

No, a witness to prove you're what I hope you are. Wish you are.

NORA

Who?

VIRGINIA

Not one? Is there not even one for each of you?

JIGEE

(*As music starts*)

I have one! Wait here, wait for me!

(*She runs off into the trees.*)

GINNA

I'm not sure—maybe—

VIRGINIA

Try! (GINNA *hurries off in another direction.* VIRGINIA *turns to* NORA) You're frightened there will be no one.

NORA

Not as frightened as you are.

VIRGINIA

But you will not even search, you will not even try—

NORA

Where? For whom? I'm wishing as hard as you are, Virginia, but who is there? Who would you call for?

(*From the trees,* ANDY *appears.*)

VIRGINIA

I didn't call a witness!

ANDY

I know who she is, I know who all three of them are—

VIRGINIA

And you've come back to see me exposed!

ANDY

Still looking for the wrong meanings. I came back to make sure you listen. (*A whistle is heard*) Enter the first witness.

NORA

(*Frightened*)

Not for me! (*Running into the trees*) Not for me!

(THE BOY *appears. His clothes are clean and neat now; his hair is slicked down. He carries a paper bag. The tinge of insolence is rooted in his embarrassment. He whistles a bit more.*)

THE BOY

Is what's-her-name around?

VIRGINIA

No.

THE BOY

Where's she gone to?

VIRGINIA

No!

THE BOY

Where's she gone to?

VIRGINIA

She is not here.

THE BOY

(*Grins*)

You don't like the smell of me.

VIRGINIA

I'm sure you won't have any trouble in finding what you came for some place else.

THE BOY

You don't rock me. I've got 'em falling over like trees and the woods're full of 'em!

VIRGINIA

This is no witness!

THE BOY

(*Angrily*)

Why not? (*Sits in a chair in the clearing, like a witness in the dock*) Attack, Your Honor!

VIRGINIA

No!

ANDY

Take the chance. Go on.

VIRGINIA

Not in front of you. I'm not on trial!

(*She moves so that she is between* ANDY *and* THE BOY.)

ANDY

But you must do the trying.

VIRGINIA

Not with him.

THE BOY

(*Laughs*)

She's just like the other one: huffy.

ANDY

Is that why you liked the other one?

THE BOY

Who said I liked her?

ANDY

Then why did you come back?

THE BOY

Oh—because I didn't have anything else to do.

VIRGINIA

A lie.

THE BOY

Because I felt like scaring her.

VIRGINIA

A lie.

THE BOY

Because she was easy, then.

VIRGINIA

Another lie.

THE BOY

Then because she was proud enough to finish what she started.

VIRGINIA

The biggest lie!

THE BOY

(*Quite simply*)

No. That's no lie.

ANDY

(*To* VIRGINIA)

Why do you want it to be?

VIRGINIA

Because it is! (*To* THE BOY) She was ashamed!

THE BOY

Afterwards, sure. But not of *me*.

VIRGINIA

She cried.

THE BOY

But not in front of me! She was scared what *I'd* think of *her!* (*Gets up*) Listen, I came back because—for Pete's sake, all that jabber and she's just a dumb, pretty, scared kid!

VIRGINIA

Pretty?

THE BOY

She's not ugly, is she? If you're not ugly, what are you? (*To* ANDY) She's too smart to understand very simple things—(*To* VIRGINIA)—and I'm not smart enough to explain. (*Looks at the paper bag*) Listen, if she turns up, give her this for me. (*Tosses it to porch steps*) If she doesn't . . . toss it in the trash can.

(*Hands in pockets, he starts off. He begins to whistle as he enters the trees, and the music picks up his notes. As* VIRGINIA *goes to pick up the bag,* NORA *enters and she hands it to her.* VIRGINIA *is turned away so that she cannot see what* NORA *takes out of the bag: a little homemade bouquet of blue asters and white cosmos.*)

VIRGINIA

Blue asters . . . and white cosmos . . .

(The music is drifting away.)

NORA

I lost that whole summer.

VIRGINIA

I thought someone had just thrown them away. *(She looks in tender wonderment at* NORA *as the girl sits on the porch steps and huddles the little bouquet close to her)* But that boy is—

NORA

(Defiantly)

Ordinary?

ANDY

He isn't. And what if he were, Virginia?

(A sharp note of music as GINNA *and* PETE *suddenly enter the clearing. He wears the summer uniform of an army officer. They stare at each other.)*

PETE

Didn't you call?

GINNA

I called for a witness . . . *(To* VIRGINIA*)* And this is the best I could do.

ANDY

Perhaps . . .

GINNA

Perhaps these trees will grow with their leaves in the ground and their roots in the sun. The witness is yours.

ANDY

(*To* PETE)

Take the chair.

(PETE *sits.*)

VIRGINIA

If it's useless—

PETE

Someone did call.

GINNA

I mentioned no name.

VIRGINIA

In that case—

ANDY

Ask the question.

VIRGINIA

Ginna—

GINNA

No!

VIRGINIA

Your witness.

GINNA

I cannot! (*She starts for the porch but* VIRGINIA *points her back to the clearing and* PETE. GINNA *stiffens, then slowly walks to him and shoots the question coldly*) Did you ever like me?

PETE

(*Factually*)

I married you, Ginna.

GINNA

(*Quickly turning*)

There!

ANDY

Objection!

GINNA

Why? What more—

VIRGINIA

He did not answer the question asked.

(*Again,* GINNA *pulls herself up and turns to him. A moment.*)

GINNA

Pete...

PETE

(*Quietly*)

I liked you, Ginna.

GINNA

(*Turns to him, would touch him—as* VIRGINIA *would*)

How could you?

PETE

You made me alive.

GINNA

I don't understand.

PETE

(*Smiles; easily*)

You didn't the other time I tried to explain. Remember? I told you I don't think life has much color of its own. It doesn't matter whether you're the world that gets in the newspapers or the world that reads them. It isn't events: a murder can be dull, a breakfast can be exciting.

GINNA *and* VIRGINIA

(*Together*)

Yes...

PETE

A few have something special, inside them. I don't know what it is. But somehow they make the same things everyone else does, they make the ordinary—exciting. They give life color . . . You did that for me.

GINNA

. . . Thank you.

PETE

(*Rises*)

Why are you thanking me? (*To* VIRGINIA) I guess I was always a little behind her. (*Starting to go*) Well, if that's all—

VIRGINIA

Wait. That ring you wear—

PETE

Oh. I married again.

(GINNA *reaches for* ANDY's *hand as support.*)

VIRGINIA

Children?

PETE

One. And another on the way.

VIRGINIA

I'm glad.

PETE

Thanks . . . Good-bye, Ginna.

GINNA

Good-bye.

(PETE *goes.*)

ANDY

You didn't destroy him.

GINNA

No. Virginia, he made out all right.

VIRGINIA

Did he? I'd heard he was back in uniform, back in a world of boys.

ANDY

But if that's his place—

GINNA

(*To* VIRGINIA)

What would be enough for you? The moon?

(*On this,* BARNEY *enters; gay, tipsy;* JIGEE *is leading him by the hand.*)

BARNEY

Oh, no, the moon is too available! The universe!

JIGEE

Ssh!

BARNEY

(Shakes her off)

All astronomical stations from Integrity to Brilliance. With local stopovers at South Charm, West Beauty, North—

(He stumbles, and ANDY *helps him into the witness seat as* JIGEE *goes to* VIRGINIA.*)*

JIGEE

I didn't know he'd be like that.

VIRGINIA

You should have by now.

BARNEY

Great way to give an impression of wisdom. *(Smiles, then suddenly yanks a bottle from his pocket and holds it up to* VIRGINIA. *She is impassive. A moment, then he shies it across the grass into the trees)* Great gesture. Ten'll get you twenty I sneak back for it later. *(To* VIRGINIA*)* Well, what's the great question you've called me here for, my dear chip off the old block of ice?

VIRGINIA

The ice is melting, but it doesn't appear that you're in any condition to see that, let alone to answer.

BARNEY

Wrong! It's when the pump is primed that it spouts. *(To* ANDY*)* How'd you do with them? Tough battle, isn't it?

ANDY

Depends on how much you care.

BARNEY

You won't win. (*To* VIRGINIA) Neither will you.

VIRGINIA

I'm trying, though. (*To* JIGEE) Your witness.

JIGEE

I can't ask when he's like that.

VIRGINIA

You must.

JIGEE

You know what he'll say.

NORA

Then why'd you fetch him?

VIRGINIA

Take the chance. Go on.

JIGEE

(*Slowly goes to* BARNEY)

Daddy . . . do you like me?

BARNEY

A man is a father; a man likes his daughter.

VIRGINIA

That's no answer, Barney!

BARNEY

Don't call me Barney, I'm your father!

VIRGINIA

Then answer, Father.

BARNEY

All your life, you've asked questions that shouldn't be asked.

VIRGINIA

All I've ever asked is one clear lasting answer to something.

BARNEY

There are no lasting answers, only lasting questions.

VIRGINIA

All right, Barney!

GINNA

No! Make him answer!

BARNEY

Answer what?

GINNA

Do you love Jigee?

JIGEE

Or Nora?

NORA

Or Ginna?

ANDY

Or Virginia?

GINNA

Yes. The answer is for all of us.

VIRGINIA

(*After a beat*)

All right. It is for all of us, then. Well?

BARNEY

Well what?

VIRGINIA

. . . Do you love me, Daddy?

BARNEY

(*Looks at her, then away, to* GINNA)

I loved you as much as you loved me. (*To* NORA) And you—as much as you'd let me. (*To* JIGEE) And you . . . (*Lamely*) Your mother was a woman who—needed much attention. There are times when a child needs more love than a parent can give.

JIGEE

(*Ripping off her glasses*)

You just think I'm a bad girl!

ANDY

No, he doesn't.

JIGEE

Then *he's* bad.

ANDY

Not "bad." Just not—

VIRGINIA

Just not perfect.

BARNEY

No. By your standards, I failed. Well, maybe I did a little with her. (*Points to* JIGEE, *then turns to* NORA) But what about you? (*To* GINNA) And you? (*To* VIRGINIA) And above all, *you*. There are times when a parent needs more love than the child gives! Did you all have to pass your anger along like a sickness? Did you have to let it turn you colder and colder with resentment? (*To* VIRGINIA) Do you have to let it freeze you into your grave?

GINNA

(*To* BARNEY)

And would you care if it did?!

NORA

You never cared!

JIGEE

You'd be glad!

ANDY

(*To* VIRGINIA)

Don't listen to them!

VIRGINIA

But they know him and you don't!

GINNA

(*To* VIRGINIA)

Is he the kind of father you want?

NORA

Is he the kind anyone wants?

BARNEY

But I'm your father!

ANDY

(*Pointing to the girls*)

Are they what you want?

GINNA

Are you what she wants?

VIRGINIA

Let me be!

ANDY

No. Not this time. Don't you know why you ask for more? Because you ask more of them.

VIRGINIA

All because of them?!

ANDY

Yes.

JIGEE

Like us.

NORA

Belong to us.

VIRGINIA

And I can belong!

ANDY

The choice is yours.

VIRGINIA

Choice! (*Pause*) This, then, is the terrible thing I felt was going to happen.

ANDY

Why terrible?

VIRGINIA

A choice should include something you want: a dream. Somehow, it never does. Somehow, it is always a choice of beggars. Why must I either fight them or take them as they are? Why must I take them at all? Why can't I be rid of them, be free, so free I could soar over those trees? That's what I dream! That's what I really choose.

ANDY

Only the stars can get up there, Virginia. Most of us aren't capable of being stars, only of refusing *not* to be. Most of us aren't even meteors. Most of us never get off the ground . . . It's not very sweet to accept that you're just another groundling.

VIRGINIA

I don't want to! I don't want to stop trying!

ANDY

(Roughly)

For a dream? The world admires those who pursue dreams. I used to admire you—until I saw you destroy anyone who wasn't the dream. Keep chasing the dream, Virginia. Keep fighting them. Anything you think, you'll think out of anger. Anything you do, you'll do out of defiance. Any hand that's offered you, you'll slap.

(Turns to go.)

VIRGINIA

(Holding out her hands)

Offer me yours!

ANDY

Would you be content with me as I am? You won't know until the day after you are content with them.

VIRGINIA

Andy!

ANDY

I've done all I can.

VIRGINIA

Don't go!

ANDY

I've never been very far away.

(He goes off up the path through the trees. She turns to BARNEY, *holding out her hands to him. There is broad space between them.)*

VIRGINIA

Offer me yours!

BARNEY

. . . They're touched with whiskey, Virginia.

VIRGINIA

I don't care!

BARNEY

(Starts to her, then stops)

They always will be.

VIRGINIA

It's all right!

BARNEY

(A longer start, then stops)

I'm too old to change.

VIRGINIA

I'm not, Daddy!

BARNEY

I meant . . . I'm too accustomed to you as a stranger.

(Embarrassed, defeated, he goes quickly into the trees. JIGEE *jams a finger into her mouth to keep from crying.)*

VIRGINIA

Don't. (NORA *puts a comforting arm around the child*) Let her be! Weep for him—not for you, not for me! He is alone; he has no one. At least, we have each other—(*A moment for her to hear the words that have tumbled out at last. The girls look at her in surprise*) We have ourselves. (*And now she slowly holds out her hands to them. Tremulously,* GINNA *and* NORA *come to her. Then, as she hugs them close, a surge of music. They step back to allow her to open her arms to* JIGEE, *who comes running across the clearing. A joyous moment; then*) You're smothering me!

NORA

(*Anxiously*)

You're not still fighting us?

VIRGINIA

No.

GINNA

But you are fighting something.

VIRGINIA

Yes . . . The end of fighting . . . because it's the end of being young. Accepting you, as you are, means accepting I can't ever be what I dreamed. (*Looks up to the trees*) No star. Not even a dream of being one. (*A last cry*) But I don't want to be a groundling! I want to rise in the air just a little, to climb, to reach a branch, even the lowest—Can't I try for that?

GINNA

Why not? An end to dreams isn't an end to hope.

VIRGINIA

Is there a difference?

GINNA

Our dream of floating free over the trees, that can never come true.

VIRGINIA

But the hope of climbing to a branch, that *is* possible!

GINNA

Yes.

JIGEE

Can't we help now?

NORA

Yes! If you'll let us.

VIRGINIA

Let you? I need you to! (*Going to the cottage*) Come! It's time for us to go!

JIGEE

All of us?

VIRGINIA

All of us together!

(*She climbs the porch steps. The light except for that on her, is fading fast. She pauses at the top*)

An end to dreams *isn't* an end to hope.

(*With an exultant gesture, she flings open the door to the cottage and turns back to the clearing*)

Ready?

(*She looks around. The girls are gone. The light begins to come back quickly, as she hastens down the steps into the clearing*)

Jigee?

(*She walks to the edge of the trees nearest the house and calls*)

Ji—gee!

(*Her answer is a musical echo—and a bath of warm, summer-green light flooding the trees near her. She crosses swiftly to the opposite side and calls*)

No—ra!

(*Again the musical echo and summer light bathing the trees. She runs to the center*)

Gin—na!

(*Again the echo and the light and the last trees clear and warm and lovely. And now the music remains to build to a resolution of the nostalgic theme. The whole stage is singing with light and air and hope.* VIRGINIA *looks around like a delighted child, and an enchanted smile breaks across her face as she says*)

It *is* pretty here!

(*She even laughs a little with delight as she turns and starts out of the clearing, up the path through the trees as*

The Curtain Falls)